Dad's Home Cooking

by
Zachary Wolinsky and Family

ISBN 978-0-9837923-2-1
Copyright 2012 by Zachary Wolinsky & Family

For more information, visit www.SummerlandPublishing.com.
Printed in the U. S. A.

Library of Congress #2012936812

Photo credits: Ms. Miranda C. Fung

A special acknowledgement of appreciation is given for the generous sponsorship gift from Northwestern Mutual Financial Network, Dallas, Texas

Dedication

For Dad's who love to cook or aspire to cook.
And for family, however you discover it, know it, and express it
- Zachary Wolinsky

If I could describe to you what drives my dad everyday with two words it would have to be Food and Family. My dad has been an inspiration throughout my life. His achievements both as a professional and a family man are humbling to me and a lot to live up to, especially in the kitchen. My dad always said cooking is a great hobby and a skill that really pays off in the future. It's something you do everyday and who doesn't like a good cook?

The kitchen was like his lab at work; his work space to perform careful measurements and procedures for a specific expected outcome, but instead of doing titrations and measuring reactions, he was synthesizing succulent briskets with creamy twice baked potatoes or concocting a savory plate of steaming seafood saffron paella.

Starting the last day of the week would always be the sweetest of my weekly awakenings. I love seeing my dad in the kitchen because I know it's a place where he can be himself and show off his character. My dad would sometimes spend a whole day preparing a meal. Some nights it would be juicy skirt steak tacos with homemade guacamole and salsa or finger lickin' BBQ baby back ribs with crispy coleslaw and bacon beans, which always made a delicious mess.

Learning to cook to me is a way of passage in the Wolinsky Family. I am so grateful to have such a talented chef for a father and hope to pass down all of his delicious recipes. I am glad he was well equipped with pots and pans while I was growing up. Now that I am living on my own I don't get to enjoy my dads cooking as frequently, but love to cook up family classics myself like chicken noodle soup. It is definitely one of my favorite hobbies as an adult. I guess the apple does not fall far from the tree. I'm so proud of my dad and aspire to be a great home cook like him. His culinary passion is what unites our family in the most wonderful way.

- Andrew Wolinsky, younger brother

Growing up as a kid, I remember walking down the street to see Zack and Andrew almost every day. I can hardly remember a time when Larry wasn't cooking. I was beginning to be interested in cooking myself at that age so I would always be asking him questions about food. He always had an answer... Like how cast iron pans are best. Or why knives that door-to-door salesmen sell aren't as nearly as good as the more expensive kind. Larry has always left the impression that he enjoys cooking for friends and family a lot. As for myself, I can always be assured that there will be a delicious meal prepared by the Wolinsky's whenever I visit them!

- Chef Jackson Kalb friend of Zach and Andrew's. 3

Acknowledgment

First of all, this book has had a long time coming. The idea came naturally to us, but collecting the recipes, finding the right publisher, revisiting all the recipes for measurements, taking photos of the dishes, and describing each dish took a long time to cook just right. My slow and low approach to life really shined through on this project and I want to express a hearty thanks to everyone who patiently supported me through the creation of this book.

We want to thank and acknowledge our family and friends who inspired Dad to cook and gave him a reason to make the neighborhood gang stop in at our house. As you will see our Dad deeply enjoyed preparing our meals that always had us wanting to come home for dinner. Our family friend Jake has grown up to be a talented chef and we love to talk about food prep with him, beaming at our success and laughing at our flops in the kitchen.

We would like to thank my Dad's parents, Nat and Muriel, who owned the incredible Well's Cheese Company in Glen Cove, New York. From Dad's parents, our Dad learned about quality meats, cheeses, and imported fine foods. From his parents he learned to appreciate simple but well prepared and served dishes. We would also like to give a sincere thanks to my maternal grandparents Glyn and Suk for they were the restaurant owners and gave Dad an opportunity to cook in a professional setting. Our Korean American roots shaped the foods we were served growing up and expanded our culinary pallet. Many times would my Dad be an emergency guest chef at my grandparent's restaurant, the Korean Sunset near the Asilomar beach in Pacific Grove, California. Here my Dad would save the day as an impromptu chef on many occasions when they were short staffed.

I would like to thank my mother for her devotion to this family effort and for her encouragement and perseverance to complete the task. She was always urging me to discuss and take notes about recipes with my Dad, whenever the opportunity existed, whether it was during a quiet afternoon in the backyard, standing around a blazing oak fire pit, or long interviews over the phone. Thanks to my amazing sister, Julia, for her critical advice and artistic watercolor paintings. Thanks to my brother, Andrew, for offering his own words about Dad and for always having a healthy appetite for testing the dishes he made.

My thanks to another family member, Gus, our Weimaraner for lovingly devouring leftovers and always enjoying the flavors no matter what was made!

Finally, we want to share a big warm thank you to our publishers, Jolinda Pizzirani and Jerry Newton of Summerland Publishing, for their unceasing patience and confidence in our dream to make this book a reality. They have always been supportive along the entire way and are living their vision of helping others make the world a better place, one page at a time.

Zachary Wolinsky

Andrew, Julia, Zach

Table of Contents

Table of Contents

When it comes to preparing a homemade meal, my father has it down to a science. Perhaps it is so because he is a scientist! An organic chemist and professor, my father's experience in the chemistry laboratory has made him comfortable in the kitchen. Or, perhaps it is because he has an innate ablility for detail and precision expecting the most of himself and the ingredients he selects.

Somehow his knowledge of science has given him an uncanny talent for culinary instincts. The way that yeast interacts with sugars and produces carbon dioxide gas and alcohol when preparing bread dough from scratch. The way that a slow cooked cut of meat allows the muscle tissues to become more tender. He has mastered numerous culinary skills for which our family, my mother, brother, sister, and I grew up enjoying.

If you asked me to name one of my fondest memories of my childhood it would surely be the cuisine that my dad lovingly cooked over the years of growing up. I can always remember so many meals that my family shared together. From an early age I knew there was something different about my parent's habit of eating in. Spending time with other families in the Pacific Palisades I began to see that, more often than not, people ate out at restaurants.

The two most important things to me are family and food. Both are essential ingredients for sustaining my happiness, health, and imagination. When I invited friends for dinner, the first thing they would notice was that we were sitting down to a homemade meal. That's right—it wasn't take-out, delivered, or deli! I did not always have an interest in the food that my parents cooked for me. It was just routine to eat at home every night.

Neither did I immediately understand the importance of family. It was not until moving away to attend the University of California, Santa Cruz that I realized how great my family and my dad's cooking is to me. Now as a young adult, cooking for myself, I often find myself calling my dad not only to say hello but to ask him a technical question regarding one of his recipes. You could count on him to save the dish!

His common sense, no nonsense approach sustained three children day to day but Saturdays, we knew, were different. Those were the days he either made a really simple dinner of leftovers or banked on all of us getting an invitation out so he wouldn't have to cook for us. We almost always had more kid friendly things to do than stay at home. Saturdays were reserved for the "Special Saturday Night

Dinners" with mom. Yes, my dad could also cook exquisite, complex, "adult only" meals as well.

There are many recipes that serve as "grown-up" recipes he prepared on Saturday night. The farmers market was frequented Saturday morning and if mom would ask him what was on the menu, he simply responded that he didn't have any idea, yet that is. It was always a surprise! "Whatever looks good" would be his reply, leaving his final dishes to be determined by what inspired him at the farmers market, the fish mark, and the grocery store.

The most fresh, local, and seasonal ingredients found would be the chosen characters in his menu. With the table set for two, candles, wine glasses, and special china and linens not usually used, the whole family enjoyed watching him prepare throughout the day. This, of course gave us great pleasure to see.

My mother was not one to be idle by any means. She and my father always enjoyed a vegetable garden. My mother raised the most magnificent baby lettuce long before baby lettuce was in vogue. Her friends delighted in the gourmet lettuce baskets she would arrange in a basket for a easy, attractive gift. Black seeded simpson, lolla rossa, red leaf, buttercrunch, romaine, and butter lettuces were just a few names I never really paid much attention to while growing up. And so, my father would use whatever was ready and mature in his meals.

My mother also contributed to the menu as she has always been the baker in our household. Homemade breads and baked goods such as pies, fruit crisps, and tarts were her specialty. Any type of fruit dessert or a chocolate dessert was their favorite conclusion to any of my father's meals.

Often after dessert and coffee or espresso, my parents would take a stroll around the block and watch the sunset. They dressed as if they were going out for dinner even though they enjoyed the comfort of their home. Neighbors would ask them where they had been, so dressed up? It was always amusing to hear them tell their friends, they simply dined at home.

And so, our collection begins with each recipe and its description written by our three siblings. You will also find original illustrations strewn about by our sister, Julia. Enjoy.

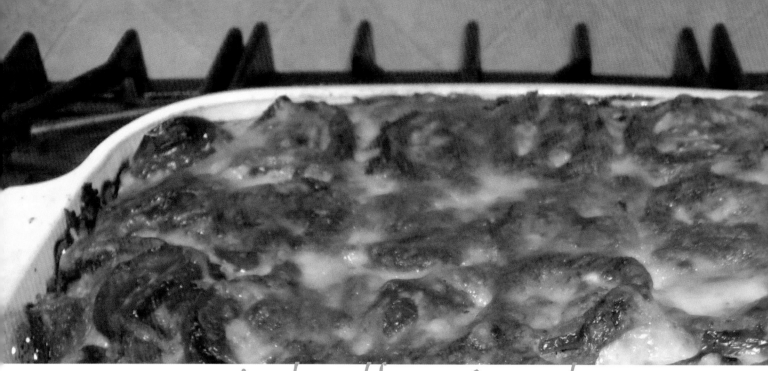

Sensational Breakfasts and Brunches

Best Bacon

INGREDIENTS:
8 to 10 slices of bacon

DIRECTIONS:

Preheat the oven 400°. Arrange the bacon evenly spaced on a large baking sheet and bake for approximately 25 minutes until crispy and well cooked. Watch the bacon closely as it can burn quickly if unattended. Remove the bacon from the baking sheet and place it on paper towels to soak up any unwanted fat.

Buy the best bacon possible. Lean, apple smoked bacon is the best and you may store it in the freezer. If it is wrapped like an accordion with either wax paper or plastic wrap, it may be removed from the freezer slice by slice. Bacon can spoil quickly in the refrigerator so if you are not going to use an entire pound of bacon rapidly, consider freezing several pieces for preparing a few strips at a time. Oven roasting the bacon is a great technique, is easy, and easy to clean up as well.

Opposite: Strata: Bacon, spinach and tomato strata.
That makes it more delicious! For vegetarian, leave
the bacon out.

Eggs in Aspic and Tarragon

We have aspics on special occasions. Aspics are simply a savory type of jello filled with meats, vegetables, or in this case a poached egg. They are a favorite Parisian meal. American are not accustomed to savory jellos. We are used to fruit gelatins with fruits or marshmellows imbedded in them or a fruit salad jello ring of some type. This is a very sophisticated way to make a savory "jello" with interesting shapes and flavors.

Eggs in Aspic

INGREDIENTS:
6 poached eggs, nicely rounded and cooled, with soft and
firm yolks (see poached egg description on page 19)
4 cups of homemade unsalted and defatted chicken stock

Clarified Aspic:
1 tsp salt
1 egg white
3 cups of mixed leaves and herbs such as celery, green
part of leeks, parsley, and tarragon
1 tbsp chopped fresh tarragon
½ tsp of pepper
4 envelopes of unflavored gelatin (3 tbsp)

DIRECTIONS:

Bring the stock to a boil in a saucepan. In another large saucepan, add 1 cup of the stock to the clarification mixture and mix well. Add the remaining stock to the mixture, mix well and bring to a boil mixing well and frequently. As soon as it comes to a strong boil, reduce to low, and boil at a low boil for 5 minutes. Do not stir or shake the mixture. Remove the pan from the heat a let it cool for 10 minutes.

Strain the broth mixture through a strainer or colander lined with cheese cloth. This will give you a very clear and beautiful liquid.

Have ready 6 clear glass ramikins and place 2 tbsp of the liquid in the bottom of each. If you want to arrange a decorative flower of steamed green leek leaves or decoratively cut steamed carrots you may do so at this time. Arrange the design and let the liquid set. Prepare the cooled poached eggs by patting them dry with a paper towel. Carefully place each egg into the ramikins and cover with the liquid. Return the ramikins to the refrigerator and allow to set for 2 hours or so. To serve, have ready plated salad plates of baby, organic greens. Carefully loosen the sides of each ramekin so that the aspic becomes loose from the glass and invert onto the greens. If there is difficulty in loosening the aspic, dip the bottom of the ramikins into hot water for 5 seconds and then invert.

Homemade Buttermilk Pancakes
with Blueberry Compote

PANCAKE INGREDIENTS:

Dry ingredients bowl :
    1½ cup sifted flour
    1 tbsp baking powder
    1 tbsp sugar

Liquid ingredients bowl:
    2 cups buttermilk
    3 egg yolks
    5 tbsp melted butter

Egg Whites bowl:
    3 egg whites

PANCAKE DIRECTIONS:

Mix the dry ingredients with a spoon. Mix the liquid ingredients with a whisk. Beat the Egg whites until fluffy and peaks form. Combine the liquid ingredients with the dry ingredients and mix well with a whisk. Fold in the egg whites and mix by folding until the batter is well incorporated. Cook pancake batter over medium heat. Serve with the best Grade A maple syrup and blueberry compote if blueberries are available.

BLUEBERRY COMPOTE INGREDIENTS:
2 cups blueberries
¼ cup of granulated sugar
1 tsp lemon juice

BLUEBERRY COMPOTE DIRECTIONS:

In a medium saucepan, add all the ingredients and bring to a boil. Reduce the heat and cook on a low boil for about 20 minutes until the liquid is evaporated and the blueberries are thick.

This buttermilk pancake recipe is the best and makes the lightest, tastiest pancakes ever. Save any leftover batter for the next day. Or make waffles and freeze them. Pancakes the next day also make a tasty dessert with jam. This is a family favorite for Sunday breakfast and we often make a double batch. We used to place blueberries directly in the batter for blueberry pancakes but in recent years we prefer the plain pancakes with the blueberry compote. They are delicious!

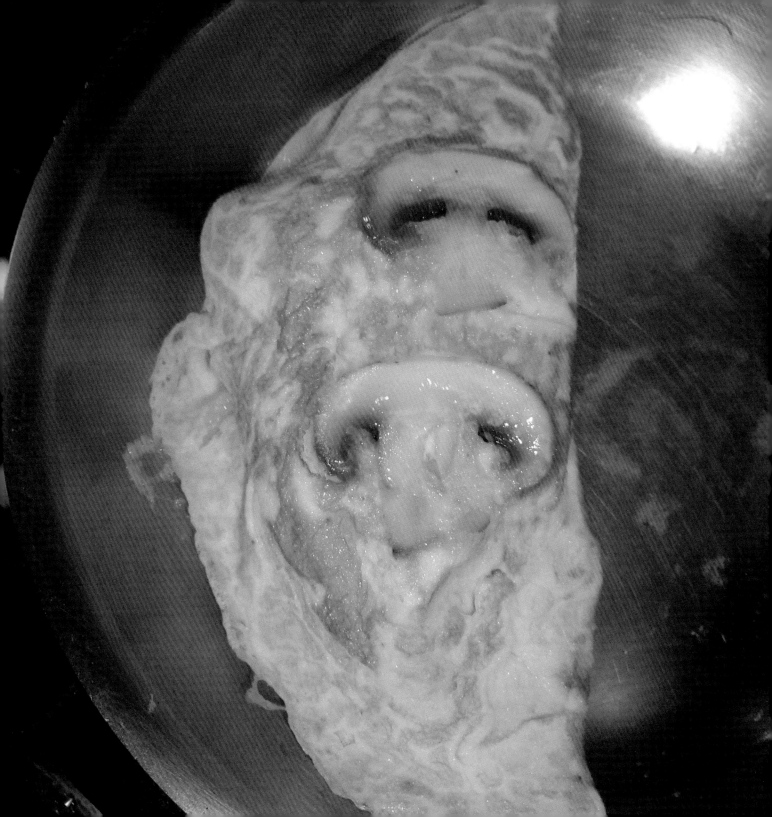

Omelet

INGREDIENTS:
1 whole egg
1 to 2 egg whites
1 mushroom sliced thin
Omelet pan well buttered

Your choice of sliced or grated cheese
Your choice of vegetables like sautéed
spinach or oven roasted vegetables
left over from dinner
Avocado slices
Fresh chopped cherry tomatoes
Your choice of fresh herbs
Your choice of either crumbled well
done bacon or chopped ham or
sausage

DIRECTIONS:

In a small bowl beat the eggs well until frothy. Heat the omelet pan on medium and arrange the sliced mushrooms decoratively in a line on the right half of the omelet pan. (If you are left handed like Dad, you would line your mushrooms on the left side of the pan in order to flip the omelet from the left to the right). Let the mushrooms cook for a few minutes making sure not to burn the butter.

Add the egg to the omelet pan and as you hold the handle, use a fork to lift the edges of cooked egg to allow for the uncooked center to swirl around and under the cooked edges so that the entire egg is evenly cooked. Turn the heat to low and add the cheese, selected vegetables, and meats. Turn the half of the omelet with the mushrooms lined toward the opposite half in order to fold and close the omelet. You will see the decorative mushrooms on the top of your omelet!

As the children in our family grew up, everyone would get up in the morning at different times and so the omelet ingredients could be left out and made to order. The trick in making an omelet or even scrambled eggs is to see if you could cook the egg and swirl it in the pan without the egg sticking all over the fork or spatula. If you work with the egg carefully as it cooks, you will not have a messy fork or spatula to clean.

You may also make an entire egg white omelet which Dad prefers. Just make sure you use enough butter or oil so the egg does not stick to the pan as it will! A great omelet can also be made for a quick dinner or even lunch and it has great protein and also allows you to use up left over vegetables.

Poached Eggs with Home Fries

POACHED EGGS INGREDIENTS:
4 cups or water in a medium saucepan
1 tsp of white vinegar
Organic brown eggs

POACHED EGGS DIRECTIONS:

Bring the water to a boil and reduce to simmering. Crack egg in a small bowl and bring the bowl to the simmering water, gently slipping the egg into the slow boiling water. Add additional 2-3 eggs and allow the egg to cook for approximately 3 minutes. With a slotted spoon, remove the egg, allowing the water to drain. Serve on top of home fried potatoes, a potato pancake, or an English muffin.

HOME FRIES INGREDIENTS:
Left over baked potatoes
Vegetable oil
Salt and pepper to taste
Optional: 1 or 2 tbsp chopped onions or red or green bell peppers

HOME FRIES DIRECTIONS:

Chop the potatoes into 1 inch cubes, leaving the potato skin on. Heat 1 tbsp vegetable oil in a sauté pan. If using onions or peppers, sauté them first in the oil over medium heat. Add the potatoes and another tablespoon of oil. On medium heat, fry the potatoes, turning them frequently to brown all sides. Add more oil if necessary. This takes about 15 minutes. The potatoes should be crispy and brown. Season as desired with salt and pepper.

This is the greatest way to use up left over potatoes. Made fresh, these home fries are great for breakfast with a poached egg on top or as a side dish for any dinner.

Danish Sausage

INGREDIENTS:
6 Danish veal sausage
1 cup water
1 tbsp vegetable oil

DIRECTIONS:

In a large frying skillet, place the water and bring to boil. Add the sausage links and steam the sausage cooking each side for 5-6 minutes each. Drain the water, keeping a lid on the sausage so they remain in the skillet and add the oil. Brown the sausage on medium heat until brown on each side. Keep turning the sausage to cook evenly so that the skins do not split.

Danish sausage is so delicious! While living in the Santa Ynez Valley, the sausage may be purchased in Solvang, the Danish city in California. We used to make 100 pounds of sausage for the annual Boy Scout Troop 41 Pancake Breakfast, held at the Presbyterian Church in Santa Ynez, California. The key is to steam the sausage to cook well and then brown them in a little vegetable oil. Do not use olive oil as the olive oil will burn.

Steel Cut Oats

INGREDIENTS:
4 cups of water in a saucepan
1 cup of McCanns Irish steel cut oats
Pinch of salt

DIRECTIONS:

Bring the water and oats to a boil and reduce to low. Cook oats for 20 minutes until oats are tender. Stir frequently. Serve with your favorite additions: brown sugar, maple syrup, honey, raisins, fresh fruit, buttermilk, or flax seed.

This old fashioned oatmeal takes more time to make but it is really worth the extra time in the morning. Put it on and stir regularily and make it your way. It is especially delicious on a cold day and the left overs keep well in the frig for another breakfast. They are chewy and hearty!

Strata

INGREDIENTS:
6 slices day old white bread with crust removed, cut into cubes
2 cup cheese (Cheddar, or Swiss, or Monterey Jack)
1 cup of mushrooms sautéed
1 cup of cooked chopped spinach
4 slices of cooked bacon chopped
Roasted red bell pepper for decoration
Asparagus spears for decoration

Custard: **2 cups whole milk**
6 eggs
Fresh grated nutmeg
½ tsp salt
¼ tsp pepper

DIRECTIONS:

Butter casserole dish and spread the bread cubes evenly. Disperse the mushrooms, spinach, and bacon pieces evenly over the bread cubes. Sprinkle with the cheese.

Mix ingredients for the custard with a whisk and pour over the vegetables, cheese, and bread crumbs. Place a few mushroom slices, peppers and asparagus in an attractive arrangement on top for decoration. Cover and refrigerate overnight. In the morning preheat the oven to 375° and bake the casserole for 45 minutes to 1 hour until puffy and golden brown.

This makes a nice breakfast or brunch meal for the entire family. When prepared the night prior, there is not much to do but bake it and eat it the next morning. You may use any vegetable or cheese you wish to use up in the refrigerator for this great dish.

Appetizers

Bruschetta

INGREDIENTS:

1 French bread bagette, sliced in ½"
diagonal slices
Olive oil, to brush bagette slices
8 Plum tomatoes, diced

2 cloves garlic, minced
1 bunch basil, chopped
3 to 5 tbsp Olive oil
Salt and pepper to taste

DIRECTIONS:

Pre-heat oven, 375°. Brush bagette slices with olive oil and toast until light brown in the oven, about 10 minutes. Cover loosely with wax-paper—do not cover or store in plastic wrap. Combine remaining ingredients and marinate about 1 to 2 hours. Just before serving, top bagette slices with tomato/basil mixture. Serve fairly soon to maintain crispness of the toast.

This is easy enough for family members to make including children. The tomatoes should be very fresh and the topping can be made an hour in advance of assembling them to maximize the flavors.

Mushroom Bruschetta

INGREDIENTS:

1 French bread bagette, sliced in ½"
diagonal slices
Olive oil, to brush bagette slices
1 lb small baby mushroom, sliced

2 cloves garlic, minced
1 bunch Italian parsley, chopped
3 to 5 tbsp olive oil
Juice of one lemon
Salt and pepper to taste

DIRECTIONS:

Pre-heat oven, 375°. Brush bagette slices with olive oil and toast until light brown in the oven, about 10 minutes. Cover loosely with wax paper (do not cover or store in plastic wrap). Combine remaining ingredients and marinate about 1 hour. Just before serving, top bagette slices with mushroom/lemon/parsley mixture. Serve fairly soon to maintain crispness of the toast.

This appetizer is lemony and light and especially good if the mushrooms have a chance to marinade for at least one hour. Use additional olive oil as you like.

25

Ceviche

INGREDIENTS:
One large non-reactive dish (glass, ceramic)
Shrimp, white fish, squid, or any seafood of your choice
10 fresh limes
Fresh cilantro
1 red onion
Celery
Chopped tomatoes
Salt

DIRECTIONS:

Quickly rinse seafood in cold water. Chop it up into little morsels. Make a mixture of lime juice, chopped cilantro, chopped celery, chopped red onion, freshly chopped tomatoes, and salt to taste. Make sure that there is enough to fully immerse the seafood. Add the seafood to the acidic mix and put in the refrigerator. Let marinade for about an hour. Serve over some tostadas or in a bowl with the juices and enjoy!

Ceviche is a fresh and exciting dish for the pallet and it is so simple to make. The fish that you include cooks when it is marinated in the lime juice. Or rather, the acids in the lime juice denature the proteins in the fish tissues and break them down. It is important to prepare ceviche in a non-reactive dish like glass or ceramic because if you were to do it in a metallic dish, the acids in the lime juice would react to the dish, giving the ceviche a metallic taste.

Curry Chicken Fillo Triangles

INGREDIENTS:
3 cups of cooked chicken, preferably all breast meat
2 tbsp curry powder
½ cup of chopped fresh cilantro
1 cup sour cream
½ tsp kosher salt
¼ tsp ground pepper
2 tbsp melted butter
½ cup chopped walnuts
1 lb prepared filo pastry sheets
½ cup melted unsalted butter

DIRECTIONS:

Mix all ingredients and taste. Season with additional curry, salt, and pepper. With lots of counter space available, spread out one sheet of the filo dough and brush with melted butter. Layer a second sheet on top of the first sheet and brush with butter. Finally add a third sheet and brush with butter. With a sharp knife, cut the sheets horizontally in half and then vertically in quarters than eighths. Cut each rectangle in half diagonally. Place a teaspoon of curry chicken mixture into each triangle and wet the filo edges, fold over and seal. Continue to make up as many triangles as you can. These may be frozen and baked for a very nice appetizer. Brush with butter and bake at 375° for 20-25 minutes.

Make four dozen of these tasty appetizers and freeze them to serve at a later dinner party or when unexpected guests arrive. They are worth the extra effort.

Gravlax

INGREDIENTS:
One fresh headless local salmon
1½ cups brown sugar
Fresh dill
½ to 1 cup of salt
String
Heavy weight (bricks do the trick)

DIRECTIONS:

Give the fish a quick rinse under some cold water and pat dry. Split the salmon open along the belly of the fish and lay down open sides up on a cooking sheet. Mix together brown sugar and salt. Spread the mixture all over the two open halves of the salmon and rub it in. Add a layer of finely chopped dill on top of the rub layer. Close the two halves back together and tie closed with some string. Take another cooking sheet with bricks or other heavy weights on it and put it on top of the fish. This will squeeze the sides together and help the salt penetrate the tissues of the salmon, thus curing it. Now it's time to put your soon to be gravlax in the refrigerator for about five days, turning it over each day. You can cover this with plastic wrap, but there really is no odor in the refrigerator. Best served on some toast or a bagel with cream cheese. It's also really good scrambled into some eggs in the morning! MmmHmm!

Curing salmon appears time consuming but it is really so, so easy—you will be pleasantly surprised how simply this can be accomplished and how tasty, clean, and wholesome home-cured salmon can be. The entire family can be involved in this process and this "cured" technique makes a great family activity.

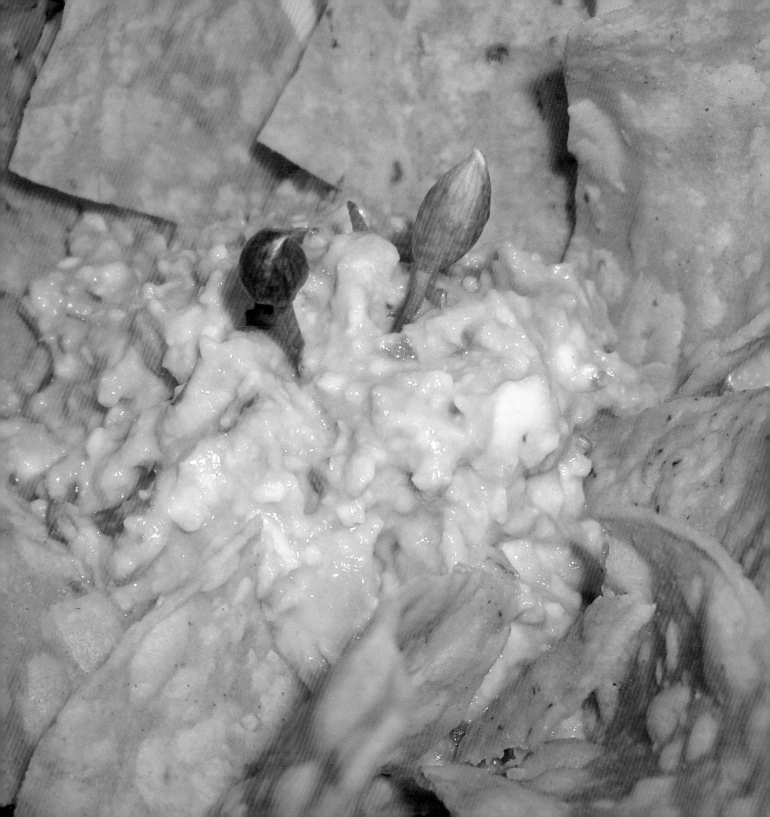

Guacamole

INGREDIENTS:
2 ripe avocados (still slightly firm but soft to touch)
Juice of 1 lemon
2 tbsp salsa
Salt and Pepper to taste
1 tbsp chopped cilantro

DIRECTIONS:

Place all ingredients in medium bowl. With clean hands, mix well.

Refrigerate up to an hour prior to serving. Serve with fresh tortilla chips.

There is something about the way that my Dad makes guacamole that's right on. I'm talking its some kind of voodoo magic that he spikes it with. It's almost like he knows what my taste buds want more than I know before I even try the dish and tell him how it is. Like many of the dishes my pops makes, he can practically do it with his eyes closed—it's his second nature at this point in his cooking career. Creamy, zesty, fresh, and a healthy accompaniment or appetizer for many a meal.

INGREDIENTS:
12 fresh oysters with shells closed: Bluepoint or Santa Barbara Hope Ranch
Crushed ice
Lemon wedges
Tomato / horseradish sauce
Cilantro / ginger sauce

DIRECTIONS:

To shuck oysters, place a kitchen towel around the oyster and using an oyster knife, pry open the shell carefully. Use the knife to separate the "oyster foot" from the shell and place the oyster loosely in the half shell. (Place the discarded, unused half shell in a sealed bag of water with a teaspoon of bleach to prevent odors in your garbage.) *(Dad says shucking oysters is very similar to elevating and extracting teeth!)*

To prepare the tomato/horseradish sauce:	2 tbsp tomato catsup
	½ tsp horseradish
	1tsp fresh lemon juice
	Ground pepper to taste
To prepare the cilantro/ginger sauce:	2 tbsp finely chopped cilantro
	½ tsp soy sauce
	1 tsp chopped fresh ginger
	1 tsp fresh lemon juice

Arrange the oysters on the half shell attractively on a platter of crushed ice, surrounded with several lemon wedges. Serve with the sauces on the side.

This is usually a dish my Dad makes for special Saturday night dinners with my mom. He likes to serve these as appetizers with a cocktail. They are good to slurp right out of the shell and taste like the ocean.

32

Salmon Cakes

INGREDIENTS:
2 cups cooked salmon, broken into small pieces
¼ cup mayonnaise
1 tbsp fresh lemon juice
2 egg whites
2 tbsp chopped fresh dill
½ tsp kosher salt
¼ tsp fresh ground pepper
Paprika
2 tbsp vegetable oil for sautéing

DIRECTIONS:

In a medium bowl combine all ingredients and using your hands or spoon, mix well. Form into four cakes, sprinkle with paprika. Heat vegetable oil in a medium skillet and pan fry the four salmon cakes until golden brown on each side. Serve on a bed of organic greens with a lemon vinaigrette.

What a great way to use leftover salmon! Our grandmother, Muriel (Dad's mom), also loved his salmon cakes and served over a bed of baby lettuce, they could be dressed up to make a lovely lunch or light dinner.

33

Tomato Salsa

INGREDIENTS:
4 ripe tomatoes, chopped
½ cup chopped cilantro
1 tsp ground cumin
½ tsp cumin seed (optional)
Juice of 1 lemon
Salt and pepper to taste

DIRECTIONS:

Mix above ingredients and refrigerate 1 hour prior to serving.

Zesty and fresh are also quite fitting words to describe my dad's homemade salsa. This is what he adds a little bit of to his guacamole. I have grown to like the cilantro so much that I will eat it all on it's own from the leftovers that my dad has when he makes salsa. It freshens the pallet. You can also add fresh finely chopped or cooked down tomatillos to elevate this salsa to another level. This is great to eat with fresh corn tortilla chips.

Opposite: Curry Chicken Salad

Soups and Salads

INGREDIENTS:
8 to 10 oz (or 1 bag) arugula
1 celery stalk
1 carrot stalk
¼ cup red bell pepper
¼ cup yellow bell pepper
½ can of baby artichokes, quartered
¼ cup chopped fresh parsley
1/2 cup of freshly grated thick shavings of parmesan cheese
Extra Virgin Olive Oil
White Balsamic Vinegar

DIRECTIONS:

Place the arugula in a large salad bowl. Chop the celery, carrot, red and yellow bell pepper and arrange on top of the arugula. Place artichoke hearts on top, sprinkle with fresh parsley and parmesan cheese shavings.. Season with salt and pepper, drizzling olive oil and vinegar on top. Toss and serve. Serves 6. Any of the vinaigrette recipes may be used.

Arugula has a delicious nutty and mildly spicy flavor on the pallet. My parents grew this every summer growing up and prepared it straight from the dirt to the plate. Parsley is a great aromatic herb and my mother loves to eat it after any meal because she likes the way it cleans the pallet and neutralizes strong flavors. Next time you are eating something strong like an Indian curry or enchiladas, try chewing on a cluster of parsley after and experience how it neutralizes the pallet.

Caprese Salad

INGREDIENTS:
4 to 6 heirloom colorful tomatoes: lemon boy, big girl, or zebra
1 to 1½ lb fresh buffalo mozzarella or burrata cheese, sliced
1 bunch fresh basil
Baby lettuce
Salt and Pepper to taste
Extra Virgin Olive Oil
Balsamic Vinegar

DIRECTIONS:

Slice tomatoes and slice the mozzarella or burrata cheese. Plate 4 salad plates with a small handful of baby greens on each plate. Arrange decoratively, the slice tomatoes and mozzarella, alternating the colorful tomatoes with a slice of cheese. Lightly salt and pepper the cheese and tomatoes. Chiffonade or finely chop the basil and sprinkle over the salad. Reserve a couple of leaves for decoration. Drizzle olive oil and vinegar over the salad to taste. Serve at room temperature.

The Caprese Salad is one of our family's all time favorite salads! We can't get enough of that ripe tomato, basil, fresh mozzarella combination in the summer! Homegrown tomatoes and basil from the garden make it extra special!

Dad's suggestion for and easy olive oil drizzlier: Use an empty vinegar bottle and fill with olive oil and label. This makes olive oil very usable in the kitchen. Shake for use for salads, to use while cooking. Extremely handy!

Classic Potato Salad

INGREDIENTS:
8 medium white boiling potatoes
2 hard boiled eggs
2 celery stalks, peeled and diced
2 tbsp Dijon mustard
½ to ¾ cup of mayonnaise
½ cup chopped fresh dill (optional)
Salt and Pepper to taste

DIRECTIONS:

In a large saucepan, fill ¾ full with salted water and bring to boil. Place whole, unpeeled potatoes into the boiling water, continue on full boil for about a minute, then reduce to medium heat for a low boil. Cook potatoes approximately 20 minutes until soft but firm. To test, use a wooden skewer or sharp knife. (Do not overcook the potatoes as they will become soft and fall apart when mixed into the salad..) Remove the potatoes from the boiling water and let cool.

Boil the eggs for 5 minutes. Remove from the heat, cooling in cold tap water. When the potatoes are cool, peel them with your fingers and slice in thin even slices. Place the potatoes into a large mixing bowl. Add the peeled and diced celery, Dijon mustard, mayonnaise, dill, and salt and pepper to taste. Mix gently to incorporate all the ingredients with the potatoes. Taste and add more salt, pepper or additional mustard and mayonnaise as you like. Sprinkle with paprika and garnish with the egg wedges. Serve well chilled.

Most recipes incorporate the egg into the salad. Our dad prefers to use the egg as a garnish rather than mixing it into the salad. This way, he especially can opt to not indulge in the egg yolk, which is high in cholesterol. Potato salad is easy to prepare and it can be done ahead of any meal. Most people think it is too much work and tend to buy potato salad as take out from the deli. The ingredients are so inexpensive that you can purchase a lot of potatoes for one small pint of take out potato salad! Make enough to have the next day.

Cole Slaw Salad

INGREDIENTS:
1 small shredded red cabbage
1 small shredded green cabbage
2 grated carrots
½ cup of sour cream or mayonnaise
1 to 2 tbsp red wine vinegar
¼ cup fresh dill, chopped
¼ cup parsley, chopped
Salt and pepper to taste
1-2 tbsp sugar (optional)

DIRECTIONS:

Combine above ingredients and mix well. Season with salt and pepper or additional vinegar or mayonnaise as desired.

Great as a side dish with barbeque or as a fresh topping on sandwiches. I can remember my parents preparing slaw and packing it up for picnics or block parties in the Pacific Palisades.

Corn Jicama Salad

INGREDIENTS:
2 ears of fresh corn, steamed, and shucked from the cob
1 stalk celery, peeled and diced
½ red bell pepper, diced
½ c jicama, diced
½ cup of black beans (canned is OK, rinse and dry)
½ cup chopped cilantro
1 tsp ground cumin
½ tsp cumin seed
1 tsp oregano leaves, fresh or dried
Salt and Pepper to Taste
Olive oil
White Balsamic Vinegar

DIRECTIONS:

Combine all the vegetables, season with salt and pepper. Drizzle with about ¼ cup olive oil and about 2 tbsp white balsamic vinegar and toss. Refrigerate 1 hour prior to serving so the flavors develop.

This is a great way to use of left over corn on the cob -- especially great in the summer when the corn is plentiful. So make extra corn just to make the salad! The jicama can be omitted if you wish. This is great with any Latin American entrée and is refreshing with any barbeque.

Curried Chicken Salad

INGREDIENTS:
2 cups chopped leftover chicken (breast, leg and thigh)
2 tbsp curry powder
4 tbsp mayonnaise
4 tbsp chopped cilantro
Salt and Pepper to taste
2 tbsp chopped toasted walnuts (optional)

DIRECTIONS:

Use leftover chicken by removing meat from the bone. Discard skin, bone and any fat. Mix all ingredients and taste for additional salt and pepper. Serve on a salad or make a sandwich.

A favorite way to use up left over salad and make a great tasting sandwich. Add toasted walnuts for extra nutrition, taste, and crunchiness. The cilantro gives additional texture and flavor.

INGREDIENTS:
2 bunches medium golden beets (6)
1 roasted red bell pepper
1 bag baby greens
Crumbled feta or goat cheese
Fresh or dried oregano, finely chopped
Salt and Pepper
Extra virgin olive oil
Vinegar of your choice: white wine or sherry

DIRECTIONS:

Heat oven 400°. Wash and scrub beets and wrap entirely with foil, place on baking sheet. Bake for 45 minutes until tender. Remove from oven and cool. Peel the beets with your fingers under the faucet of the kitchen sink and place in a zip-lock bag until ready for use.

Roast the bell pepper on the stove top—blacken entirely and place in a brown paper bag to "sweat". Peel the blackened skin off the pepper with your fingers rinsing well under the kitchen sink faucet. Remove the seed also using your fingers and place in a zip-lock bag until ready for use. In a medium salad bowl, place the baby greens. Chop or slice the golden beets and roasted red pepper and arrange on the greens. Top with crumbled feta cheese or goat cheese.

Sprinkle with freshly chopped oregano or dried oregano. Drizzle with olive oil and white wine vinegar. Salt and pepper to taste and toss. Serve 4-6.

Our family loves golden beets! My mother even makes pickled beets with oregano. One of the things we welcome every spring from our garden in California is the wild oregano which comes back annually to greet us. It is a hearty herb which survives the heat or rain and when cut back to the ground, makes its appearance yearly regardless of the weather. It is a survivor herb and very independent! We dry this herb every year to make the best homegrown stash of oregano you can imagine. The favor of the fresh oregano is divine in salads or makes an incredible additional flavor any barbecued meat.

42

GREEK SALAD INGREDIENTS:
1 large bunch of romaine lettuce
1 English cucumber
20 to 30 cherry tomatoes
1 roasted red pepper
½ French feta cheese
Fresh or dried oregano
Greek Calamata olives, pitted
Lemon vinaigrette

LEMON VINAIGRETTE INGREDIENTS:
¼ fresh orange or lemon juice
1 tsp white wine vinegar
1 tbsp Dijon mustard
1 clove garlic (smashed)
½ cup of virgin olive oil
1 tsp honey
Salt and pepper to taste

DIRECTIONS:

Wash and pat dry the romaine lettuce leaves. Chop and place in a large salad bowl. Slice and chop the cucumber, cherry tomatoes and roasted pepper. Place on top of the lettuce in the bowl. Crumble the feta cheese on top. Sprinkle oregano over the salad and top with pitted calamata olives. Toss with lemon vinaigrette and serve. Serves 6.

LEMON VINAIGRETTE DIRECTIONS:

Combine first four ingredients and whisk in the olive oil and honey. Season as desired.

(Balsamic vinegar or white balsamic vinegar may be substituted for the orange or lemon juice. Adjust the seasoning to your taste, making it either tarter by increasing the acidity or sweeter by increasing the honey or sweetener of choice.)

Dad mixes the vinaigrette directly in a large bowl with a whisk. He rinses the lettuce and keeps it chilled in the refrigerator until ready to toss. Don't forget to take the clove of garlic out prior to mixing. None of us like to bite down on a raw piece of garlic but the flavor of the garlic is extracted from the clove by the acid of the lemon or orange juice.

Lemon Vinaigrette

43

Spinach and Pear Salad

INGREDIENTS:
1 bag baby spinach
1 celery stalk, chopped
1 carrot, chopped
2 poached bosc pears
Blue Cheese, crumbled

DIRECTIONS:

Place baby spinach in a large bowl, top with chopped celery, carrots, sliced pears. Top with crumbled blue cheese and dress with an orange vinaigrette.

Such a refreshing salad, it will wake up your family members and guests at the dinner table. Sometimes my Dad will toss in some oven roasted or candied pecans for their healthy fats and crunchy texture. Wait 'til you see the glow in the faces across the dinner table that ensue from eating this enlivening salad together.

Dad's Delicious Chicken Soup

INGREDIENTS:

Whole free-range, locally raised, grain-fed chicken
5 or so celery stalks, washed
5 large carrots sliced

2 medium sized yellow onions
1 large fennel bulb
Salt
Peppercorn

DIRECTIONS:

Wash the celery, carrots and fennel bulb. Slice the celery at an angle at whatever length you prefer. Do the same for the carrots, but make sure to not cut them too thick. Peel onions, half, and then cut halves into fourths because you want big pieces of onion. Do the same for the fennel, but remove the fennel stalks and cut out the bottom core of the bulb. Pull off the fennel leaves, the part that looks similar to dill *(DO NOT THROW AWAY THE SCRAPS! You can keep the celery, carrot, onion skin, and fennel scraps to make a stock another time.)*

Next, wash and clean out the chicken and put it into your large pot. Put all of the cut up vegetables over and around the chicken in the pot. Fill the pot with water until everything is just submerged or a little over. Add salt and pepper. Bring to a boil and then simmer for a good 2 hours. The longer it simmers, the better the soup will be. Give it a taste and decide whether you like more salt and pepper. Serve with egg noodles or matzo balls.

This recipe is so easy to make and very affordable, especially if you know your farmer. It's simple, it's hardy, and if you make a big pot of soup you get to enjoy it with friends and family because it will go a long way. My dad always makes this soup during the winter season when it's cold outside and all you need to thaw from the cold is a big bowl of soup. He swears by the powers of the stock as a super tea because it's got the nutrients and essence of all of the ingredients. Boiling the bones is the secret to longevity, good health, and gives the stock a rich and flavorful taste. There is something so special about the ceremony of eating chicken soup—the way it nourishes my hunger and feeds my soul. I always make a hearty sized pot of this soup and look forward to sharing it with others.

Lentil Soup

INGREDIENTS:
2 tbsp olive oil
1 tbsp butter
2 medium onions, peeled and chopped
4 celery stalks, peeled and chopped
4 carrots, peeled, and chopped
2 tbsp dried thyme
2 bay leaves
6 to 8 cups of low-salt chicken or vegetable stock
1 16 oz bag of lentils (green, brown, or pink)
Salt and pepper to taste

DIRECTIONS:

Heat the olive oil and butter in a large soup pot. Saute the onions, celery, and carrots in the oil and butter to "sweat" the vegetables about 5 minutes. Add the thyme and bay leaves and sauté 2 minutes more. Add the chicken stock, lentils and bring to a boil. Turn down heat to simmer for approximately 1 hour. Check to see if additional water or stock if needed. Season with salt and pepper to taste. Serves 6.

Like the split pea soup, this recipe is really simple and easy to make. It nourishes your body and soul and makes the whole family happy. It freezes well too if you make a lot for a latter time.

Mushroom Barley Soup

INGREDIENTS:
2 tbsp olive oil
1 tbsp butter
2 medium onions, peeled and chopped
2 lbs mixed mushrooms
2 tbsp dried thyme
2 bay leaves
6 to 8 cups of low-salt chicken or vegetable stock
1 16 oz bag of barley
Salt and Pepper to taste

DIRECTIONS:

Heat the olive oil and butter in a large soup pot. Sauté the onions and mushrooms in the oil and butter to "sweat" the vegetables about 5 minutes. Add the thyme and bay leaves and sauté 2 minutes more. Add the chicken stock, barley and bring to a boil. Turn down heat to simmer for approximately 1 hour. Check and add additional water or stock if needed. Season with salt and pepper to taste. Serves 6.

Another rich and delicious soup that is amazing on warm summer evenings or cold winter days. A great way to use old rock hard stale bread is to put it into your soup bowl and pour the soup over it. The stale bread becomes unbelievable tender and sops up the entire flavor. I recommend using old French bread.

Potato Leek Soup

INGREDIENTS:
2 good-sized leeks
3 large Yukon gold potatoes *(It is also fun to try this recipe with different kinds of potatoes)*
1 large onion
2 large cloves of garlic
2 quarts of your scrap stock or any stock you like
Fresh Rosemary from the backyard
Heavy cream (optional)
Olive oil
Salt
Pepper

DIRECTIONS:

Cut of the green tops off the leeks so that the cut end is like an arrow point. This way you get the inner part of the leek that extends higher up the stalk. Halve the leeks, put halves side by side, and chop thinly. Slice the potatoes thinly. Dice onions and garlicup

Using a decent sized pot, sauté the leek and the onion until they are both softened. Add the sliced potatoes and diced garlic and let sauté for a few more minutes. Add 2 quarts of stock until the ingredients are just covered with liquid. Add freshly chopped rosemary and a couple teaspoons of salt and freshly ground pepper.

Simmer until the potatoes are softened. Drain and use a potato masher to break up the potatoes. Don't mash too much so that potatoes keep a chunky consistency to the soup. Serve with some fresh sourdough and enjoy!

> *Given potatoes and leeks as the base for this soup, it is naturally rich and can be even richer depending on your personal preference of the amount of cream you like. Leeks taste similar to the onion, but have a unique quality all on their own. This is a springtime classic that keeps you cozy during April showers. Serve with slices of fresh baguette to dip and pour soup over in your bowl.*

After a fun day in the snow, a nice bowl of delicious
split pea soup really hits the spot!

50

Split Pea Soup

INGREDIENTS:
1 16 oz bag of split peas
2 tbsp olive oil
1 tbsp butter
2 medium onions, peeled and chopped
4 celery stalks, peeled and chopped
4 carrots, peeled, and chopped
2 tbsp dried thyme
2 bay leaves
6 to 8 cups of low-salt chicken or vegetable stock
1 ham bone (left over from a spiral ham)
Salt and pepper to taste

DIRECTIONS:

Heat the olive oil and butter in a large soup pot. Saute the onions, celery, and carrots in the oil to "sweat" the vegetables about 5 minutes. Add the thyme and bay leaves and sauté 2 minutes more. Add the chicken stock, split peas, and ham bone and bring to a boil. Turn heat down to simmer for approximately 1 hour. Check and add additional water if needed. Season with salt and pepper to taste. Serves 6.

This is another classic dish that my Dad makes with all the right fixings and spices. There is a heartiness that comes from the addition of the ham bone. Adding bones in soups creates a special richness to the broth and has also been shown to be beneficial to one's health, especially if the animal which the bone comes from lived a happy and healthy life. Bay leaf is strong so you only need a couple of leaves and they give the soup a distinct character. I associate bay leaves with my Dad's soups so much that I am reminded of him when I walk among the Laurel Bay's trees of Wilder Ranch or Pogonip Park adjacent to UCSC's beautiful campus.

Split Pea Soup With Braised Short Ribs

INGREDIENTS:
8 thick and lean English beef short ribs
Kosher salt and pepper
2 tbsp olive oil
1 onion
6 carrots, peeled and sliced
3 parsnips, peeled and sliced
3 cloves of garlic, chopped finely
1 lb yellow split peas
1 bunch of dill

DIRECTIONS:

Season the short ribs with salt and pepper. In a large soup pan, heat 1 tbsp olive oil and brown the short ribs, placing only a few at a time in the pot to brown. Turn on all sides to brown evenly—this takes about 8 minutes. Remove short ribs from the pan. Add 1 tbsp olive oil and sauté the onions until brown and add the remaining vegetables and garlicup Sauté another 2 minutes and add the short ribs back to the pot. Add the yellow split peas. Place half the bunch of dill on top and add with enough water to entirely cover the ingredients. Bring to a boil. Reduce to low and cook on low for approximately 1 hour.   Taste and season with salt and pepper as needed.

This is a wonderful hearty soup that can be made up a day in advance if you know you have no time to cook on a particular day. Actually the flavors and consistency improve with a days time. Make a salad and have some fresh crusty bread to enjoy with. This recipe feeds a family and more. There is always enough to take to school of work for the next day's lunch!

Vegetable Scrap Soup

INGREDIENTS:
Fennel scraps
Carrot scraps
Celery scraps
Onion scraps and skins
Garlic scraps
Left over mushroom stems
Kale stems and scraps
Broccoli scraps
Any other scraps that you froze away for later
Rosemary, oregano, and any herbs you like

DIRECTIONS:

Place all of the vegetable scraps that you can muster into a large pot and fill with water until it is an inch or so past the point at which all the ingredients begin to float.

Bring to boil and simmer for 2 hours—the longer the better. Add salt and pepper to taste and strain.

This soup stock is a great way to really make the most of your veggies and scraps from previous dishes. A good friend and teacher, Jasper Clementine, inspired me to do this and it is a practice that resembles my Dad's habit of repurposing leftovers from previously enjoyed meals. Thanks to the invention of the freezer it doesn't require any time sensitive commitment either. What you can do is take any scraps from making a dish and just keep a bag or container in the freezer to collect the scraps in. Over time, you will have enough for a potentially rich and healthy stock using resources that would otherwise be thrown away or composted. As a really basic dish, I like to pour a stock like this over some wild rice and enjoy it with some fresh ground pepper on top.

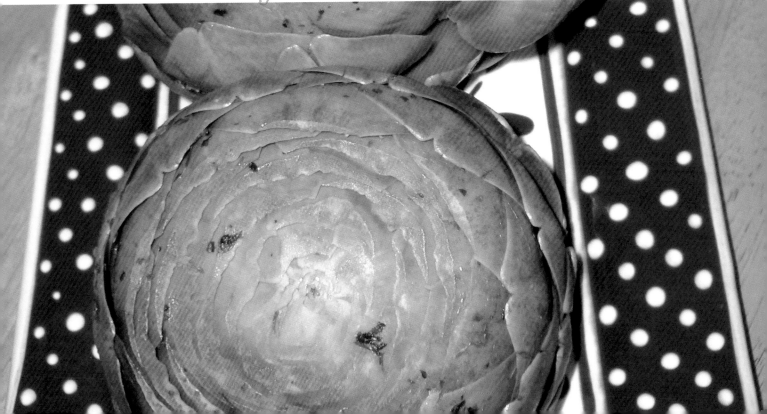

Vegetables and Side Dishes

Asparagus Three Ways

DIRECTIONS:

Steamed: 1 bunch asparagus peeled and prepared

To prepare the asparagus, cut a couple of inches off the bottoms to remove the white stem. With a carrot peeler, peel the cut stem around the bottom. Place the asparagus in a steamer and steam for 3-4 minutes until the spears are tender and bright green. Remove from the steamer and immediately submerse in ice water to prevent further cooking.

Steamed asparagus is great hot or cold. To reheat prior to dinner, simply heat in the microwave for 1 minute and serve. Cold or room temperature asparagus is great on a salad or with cold poached salmon.

Oven-Roasted: 1 bunch asparagus, peeled and prepared as above
Olive Oil
½ lemon
Salt and pepper

Preheat oven to 375°. To prepare the asparagus, cut a couple of inches off the bottoms to remove the white stem. With a carrot peeler, peel the cut stem around the bottom. Place asparagus spears on an oiled baking sheet and drizzle with olive oil. Squeeze half a lemon over the asparagus and season with salt and pepper. Bake for 40 minutes.

Grilled Asparagus: 1 bunch asparagus, peeled and prepared as above
Olive Oil
½ lemon
Salt and pepper

With a carrot peeler, peel the cut stem around the bottom. Place asparagus spears on an oiled baking sheet and drizzle with olive oil. Squeeze half a lemon over the asparagus and season with salt and pepper. Grill over a hot grill for 2 minutes on each side.

Asparagus, a hallmark of spring, is colorful and tasty. Be sure to prepare them properly by peeling the ends a couple of inches to reveal the inner light color. The cooking is improved and the fibrous ends are eliminated. Don't worry if your urine has an unsual odor as the compound responsible is methanethiol and only some of us (22%) can detect the odor.

Grilled Vegetables

INGREDIENTS:
Green bell pepper
Red sweet pepper
Orange or yellow bell pepper
Medium sized mushroom
Zucchini cut in large ½" slices
Sweet purple onions, cut into large chunky pieces
Cherry tomatoes

DIRECTIONS:

Cut all the vegetables into large pieces. The bell peppers may be quartered and the cut in half to make 8 pieces for each pepper. Using either metal skewers or water soaked wooden skewers, spear each vegetable until each skewer is full of the same vegetable. Remember not to over load the skewer—leave room at each end for you to handle and turn the skewer while grilling. (We prefer one type of vegetable on each skewer rather than alternating the vegetables as is customarily done. The reason for this is the vegetables each cook at different times and this way the grill time is customized for the vegetables. For example, the tomatoes cook quicker than the peppers and therefore if cooked in stages all the tomatoes may be removed from the grill at the same time, if they are all on one skewer.)

After all the vegetables are skewered, sprinkle with a little salt and pepper and baste with olive oil. Place all the skewers on the grill and cook until done—15-20 minutes for the peppers and onions and less for the mushrooms and tomatoes (Grill whole or halved vegetables work well directly on the grill too).

Vegetables grilled on the barbeque incur extra flavor. Tossed first with extra virgin olive oil and fresh herbs, this technique may include many vegetables and is a fabulous way of using up vegetables left in the refrigerator bin for a few days. Keep them in large pieces, halved or whole for grilling.

Oven Roasted Vegetables

INGREDIENTS:
2 sweet red bell peppers
1 green bell pepper
½ lb of mushroom
1 sweet red onion
2 zucchini
2 yellow squash
½ cup of olive oil
Fresh rosemary sprigs
2 peeled cloves of garlic
Salt and pepper to taste

DIRECTIONS:

Preheat oven 375°

In a large bowl combine all vegetables which have been quartered or halved, depending on your preference. Sprinkle with the salt and pepper and olive oil. Mix well by hand and position all vegetables on an oiled baking sheet. Bake for 1 hour or until vegetables are lightly brown and tender.

This is a great way to prepare vegetables when the oven is on. With a baking sheet, they take up a minimal vertical height in the oven and may be cooking while a chicken is roasting. Also, it is a great way to use up vegetables in the refrigerator that are aging. You may oven roast any vegetable you wish and flavor with other herbs are well.

Roasted Red Bell Peppers

INGREDIENTS:
4 red sweet bell peppers (yellow or orange may be used as well)
1 medium brown paper bag
½ cup olive oil
¼ tsp salt
⅛ tsp pepper
2 smashed garlic cloves
A few dashes of red wine vinegar

DIRECTIONS:

Turn four gas burners on high and position each pepper directly on the grill. (Turn the hood vent on and open the windows as grilling these can set off the smoke alarm in the house.)

Blacken each side of the peppers until they are entirely charred. Place them in the brown paper bag to "sweat." This allows the skins to peel off easily. Remove the skins and seeds from each pepper and quarter them by hand. Place all the peppers in a glass bowl, cover with olive oil, salt, pepper, and the garlic cloves and turn to mix well. Splash a few dashes of red wine vinegar into the mixture. Marinade a few hours prior to use for the best flavor. (To smash the garlic clove: peel the clove and with a butcher knife pound the clove on the counter top or cutting board to smash the clove, releasing the juice and flavors.)

These peppers are the greatest and may be used in a sandwich, salad, or on top of a pizza. They are very versatile and add color and flavor to almost anything.

Sautéed Spinach

INGREDIENTS:
1 bag of pre-washed baby spinach
2 tbsp olive oil
½ tsp salt
¼ tsp pepper
¼ tsp fresh grated nutmeg

DIRECTIONS:

In a sauté pan, heat the olive oil. Add the spinach and sauté on high for 2 minutes, mixing well. Sprinkle with salt, pepper, and grated nutmeg, and mix well.

This is really fast food at its best. Sautéed spinach is healthy and takes only a couple of minutes to make. The fresh grated nutmeg is a must for the unique flavor. Any leftovers may be used in an omelet the next day. This is a very elegant side vegetable that goes with just about any main dish.

Steamed Artichokes

INGREDIENTS:
3 large artichokes
4 cups water
¼ olive oil
1 tbsp dried oregano
1 tbsp dried basil
1 tsp dried thyme
1 tsp kosher salt
¼ tsp pepper

DIRECTIONS:

Prepare the artichokes by slicing off the stem close to the bottom and horizontally cut the top to remove the upper sharp spines on the leaves. In a large kettle, bring the water, olive oil, and remaining spices to a boil. Gently lower the artichokes into the boiling water and reduce to simmer or a slow boil. Simmer for approximately 45 minutes to an hour or until the artichokes are tender to a skewer insertion. Remove from the pan and allow to cool to room temperature.

To enjoy, remove each leave and using your teeth, remove the tasty flesh from the inner bottom portion of the leave. Continue to eat, removing the leaves until the heart is reached. With a spoon, remove the furry covering over the bottom to expose the heart. Share the heart with someone very special.

The best artichokes come from Lompoc, California and they are so tender, sweet and large! Sometimes they require extra time to cook but the wait is worthwhile. Some people like to dip the leaves in mayonnaise or butter but we prefer the tasty leaves by themselves and we also like the avoid the extra calories of the dip. They make a great appetizer and are fun to share. Lompoc also grows some beautiful baby purple artichokes as well.

Couscous

INGREDIENTS:
1 cup couscous
1 ¾ cup water or chicken broth
1 tbsp butter
2 tbsp dried currants and/or toasted slivered almonds (optional)

DIRECTIONS:

Bring the water or chicken broth and butter to a boil in a saucepan. Remove from the heat and add the couscous and currants. Mix well and cover with the lid for five minutes until the liquid is absorbed. Mix with a fork before serving.

This is the epitome of fast food! If you need a starch to accompany a meal there is nothing quite as fast and wholesome as couscous which is cracked wheat. You may add currants and toasted almonds to change the texture and character.

Mushroom Risotto

INGREDIENTS:
1 large fresh Boletus Edulis (Porcini mushroom)
3 to 5 button mushrooms
½ onion
Chicken broth
1 cup Arborio rice
Parmesan cheese (grated)
Olive oil

DIRECTIONS:

Dice half of an onion and sauté in saucepan with a little olive oil until the onion is clearer and softened. Add chopped porcini and button mushrooms and sauté with onions for a few minutes.

While this is sautéing, heat up some chicken broth. Add 1 cup of Arborio rice and little more olive oil. Sauté for a couple minutes until the rice begins to clear. Make sure that all of the rice is consistently covered with oil.

Next, add warmed chicken broth in small increments to the rice and stir often.

When rice is cooked, serve and garnish with Parmesan cheese.

It could be said that in cooking risotto, one learns of the ways of patience and persistence. And one of the greatest times of the year to wait to eat this dish is in the fall, when the Boletus edulis, commonly known as the porcini mushroom, emerges fresh from the forest floor. The porcini is a west coast delicacy and here in California a slow walk through the woods and a keen eye may present you with one of these gorgeous gifts. Some can grow bigger than your head! My Dad loves to cook with this mushroom and this risotto is some of the finest Italian comfort food he makes. As simple as sautéing the ingredients and gradually adding broth, this dish promises richness in every bite. The finished risotto should be creamy in texture and somewhat runny.

Pesto

INGREDIENTS:
3 cups of fresh basil
1 cup of fresh Italian parsley
1 cup of pine nuts or walnuts
1 cup of freshly grated parmesan cheese

2 cloves of garlic, smashed
½ to 1 cup of extra virgin olive oil
1 tsp salt
¼ tsp pepper

DIRECTIONS:

In a food processor, with the chopping wheel inserted, place the roughly chopped basil and parsley, pine nuts, parmesan cheese, garlic, salt and pepper. Pulse the ingredients to chop and add the olive oil through the lid spout as the food processor is mixing. Add enough olive oil for the mixture to become a smooth paste. Taste and adjust the seasoning — more salt, pepper or more cheese. Mix with the pasta of your choice.

Pesto is an all time favorite of our family! We can't get enough of it during the summer when fresh basil is at its peak season. And guess what? It doesn't even have to be cooked! The bright green color is amazing. Use about a cup of pesto with 4 cups of cooked pasta of your choice (we like bow-ties) and toss. Add extra olive oil as you are tossing and be sure to taste it and season as needed. Sprinkle more freshly grated parmesan cheese. You may also freeze the pesto by storing in a glass jar filled only about ¾ full, topping with a thin layer of olive oil. This makes a great surprise to take out and use with any leftover cooked pasta that you may have.

Rice Pilaf

INGREDIENTS:
⅛ lb thin pasta like angel hair or spaghettini
1½ cup of long grain rice
1 tbsp olive oil
1 tbsp butter
2¾ cup chicken broth

DIRECTIONS:

In a medium saucepan, heat the olive oil and butter. With your hands, break up the pasta into 1 inch pieces, throwing them into the olive oil and butter. On medium heat, sauté the pasta until it becomes coated with the oil. Add the rice and sauté the rice with the pasta until the rice becomes brown. Heat the chicken broth in the microwave until it is warm (about a 1 minute). Pour hot broth into the rice/pasta mixture, mixing well. Bring to a boil and then reduce to low. Cook with the lid on for approximately 20 minutes.

This is one of my favorite dishes that my dad makes because it was one of the first of his dishes I learned to cook. As a matter of fact, I acquired the trail-name, Grandma Pilaf, in summer of 2010 when I was cooking dinner for my tribe in the Yollie Bolly Wilderness of Northern California. It was my first time making pilaf over an open fire in one giant pot and by 9 o'clock after a long day of hiking, tummies were growling. It was dark by the time we ate (even amidst extended hours of sun) and everyone was practically starving. But hey, it turned out alright and everyone liked it sure enough. To this day I will never live down the nickname Pilaf.

Saffron Risotto

INGREDIENTS:
1 cup of Arborio rice
2 cups chicken broth
½ onion, chopped finely
Olive oil
Turmeric
Saffron

DIRECTIONS:

Using a small cooking pot, begin by sautéing half of an onion in some olive oil. After about 5 minutes of sautéing, add 1 cup of Arborio rice and stir around until the grains are coated with olive oil. Let the starch of the outer part of the rice cook for 7 minutes on medium heat. Heat up 2½ cups of chicken broth so that it is nearly boiling. After letting the rice cook, add the chicken broth in quarter cup increments every 5 minutes or so, adding more as the liquid is absorbed (about 25 minutes). Be careful when you first add the broth as it may excitedly boil in the pot. Add turmeric and stir to give the risotto a beautiful yellow color. Add saffron and stir. Serve and enjoy!

Saffron is the stamen of the crocus and is highly valued and an expensive spice. It imparts an interesting and sometimes not quite identifiable flavor, certainly a flavor that the kids in our family may not readily identify. It is an intense flavor and only a few strands are required to color and beautifully flavor Arborio rice.

Opposite: Cioppino

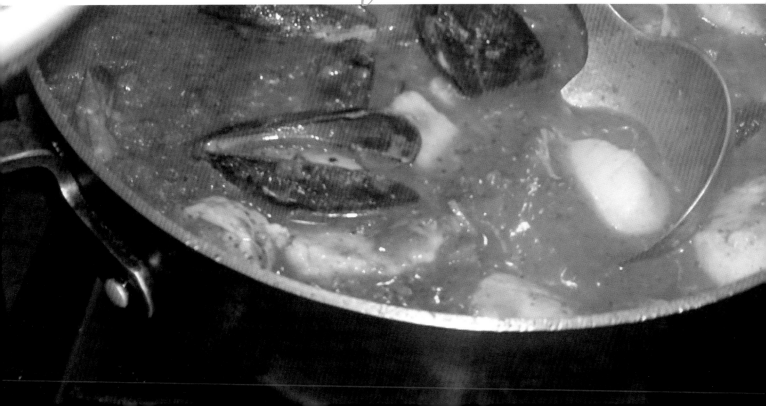

Family Dinners

Baby Back Ribs

INGREDIENTS:
2 racks of baby back pork ribs
Rub: 1 cup granulated sugar
3 tbsp chili powder
1 tbsp ground cumin
1 tbsp ground oregano
2 tbsp kosher salt
1 tsp pepper
1 tbsp garlic powder
1 tbsp paprika
3 tbsp ground cinnamon
Olive oil

DIRECTIONS:

Rinse ribs in cold water and pat dry. Mix the ingredients for the rub and rub onto the ribs. Drizzle lightly with olive oil.

Start a Santa Maria barbecue pit with red oak wood and allow to mature for 30 minutes. Lower the grill to approximately 4 inches from the flame and grill the ribs for about 15 minutes on each side, watching and turning frequently to prevent burning the ribs.

If the ribs begin to burn, raise the grill or cover with foil.

Santa Maria Barbecue is a specialty of the central coast of California. You will see these barbeques on the main streets of Santa Maria, California on the weekend. The barbeque pit is a large metal box on a stand with a grill that can be raised manually with a winding wire. The red oak is native to California and imparts a wonderful flavor to any meat that you grill. It provides a distinct flavor to the meat.

Brisket with Kasha Varnishkes

BRISKET INGREDIENTS:
1 to 2 lbs of Beef Brisket
3 to 4 carrots
3 to 4 parsnips
4 cloves of garlic
3 yellow onions
Vegetable oil
Small can of tomato paste
Salt and pepper

KASHA VARNISHKES INGREDIENTS:
1 cup medium sized kasha buckwheat
   grains
1 cup small bowtie pasta
2 cups of chicken stock
2 tbsp of vegetable oil
1 yellow onion
1 egg well beaten
Salt and Pepper

BRISKET DIRECTIONS:

Rinse the beef brisket under cold water and pat dry with a towel. Season with salt and pepper. Using a little bit of vegetable oil (don't use olive oil because it will burn) in a large dutch oven or ceramic casserole pan, brown the meat giving each side about 5 to 7 minutes of cooking. Remove meat from the pan. Add yellow onions thinly sliced and sauté until browned. While onions cook, dice up carrots, parsnips, and garlic and add to pan after onions are a little browned. When veggies are nearly thoroughly cooked, put meat back into pan atop veggies and add just enough water to the pan so that the liquid is just level with the meat, not submersing it. This will braise the meat. Stir in 1 small can of tomato paste and simmer over on low heat for about 1½ hours. Cooking can also be done for the same amount of time in the oven at 325°. After the meat is cooked and simmered, slice the meat against the grain into half inch slices.

KASHA VARNISHKES DIRECTIONS:

First add the cup of kasha to the beaten egg and mix so that all of the kasha grains are covered. Using a heated non-stick pan, add the egg washed kasha and stir around until the egg is dry and the grains are mostly separate. Set kasha aside. Begin the process of cooking the bows by bringing salted water to a boil. In a medium sized pot, heat vegetable oil and sauté the diced yellow onion. Add chicken stock and bring to a boil. Stir in the kasha, a pinch of kosher salt, and some freshly ground pepper. Cook on low heat for about 10 minutes, stirring occasionally, until the kasha is tender. As the kasha is cooking, cook the small bowtie pasta until it is al dente. Drain and mix into the kasha.

Dad's brisket is what all of us crave when we are off to college. Once Andrew said he even woke up dreaming about it! The home smells so wonderful as he prepares the meal. This is definitely a family classic!

Chicken a la Marbella

INGREDIENTS:

1 whole organic cut up chicken
2 legs
2 thighs
1 cup olive oil
⅓ cup red wine vinegar
4 clove garlic, smashed
2 tbsp dried oregano
3 bay leaves
1 small jar of capers, rinsed and drained

1 large jar of Spanish olives, rinsed and drained
2 cups of dried prunes
Salt and pepper
1 cup light brown sugar
1 cup chardonnay
1 cup fresh cilantro, chopped and a few sprigs for garnish
Long grain rice

DIRECTIONS:

Rinse the chicken and pat dry. Prepare the marinade by mixing all ingredients up to the salt and pepper and stir well. Submerge the chicken pieces and turn to coat the chicken well with the marinade. Cover in a large bowl and marinade overnight.

The next day: preheat the oven 375°. Remove the chicken from the marinade and arrange in a large baking dish. Sprinkle 1 cup of brown sugar and then pour the wine over the chicken. Bake for 1 hour until golden brown. Serve with white long grain rice and chopped cilantro and the vegetable of your choice.

> *This is a long-time favorite recipe for many family gatherings at home or on the road. This travels well and may be served at room temperature. We have taken it to the beach or to another friend's home to serve as a very elegant and tasty dinner. If you are busy working, the fact that it is marinated and prepared the night before means you simply turn on the oven and place it in to bake when you return home. For working parents, even a teenager can get a head start on dinner before the family arrives for dinner. (Just make sure the wine isn't available to them!)*
>
> *This is one of our favorite recipes in our collection and is requested by the family on so many occasions. As we say, Chicken Marbella, what the Hella!*

Chicken Enchiladas

INGREDIENTS:

Already cooked or left over chicken
  meat (as much as you like)

Vegetable oil

1 onion

1 cup of diced chiles (great with either
  Anaheim or Pasilla peppers)

Ancho chile powder (from dried
  Poblano peppers)

Chicken broth

Tomato sauce

Jack Cheese

Corn Tortillas

2 small cans of black olives

Chile powder

Salt

Pepper

DIRECTIONS:

    Begin by making homemade enchilada sauce simply by mixing 2 cups of chicken broth, 1 cup of tomato sauce, and some chile powder together in a bowl Sauté onion in vegetable oil until it becomes translucent and soft. Add shredded chicken meat to the onions and sauté until browned. Add the cup of diced chiles and a pinch of ancho chile powder to add some heat. Add salt and pepper to taste.

    Next, add two thirds of the homemade enchilada sauce to the pan and let simmer on low for about 10 minutes. Heat up another pan with remaining enchilada sauce. While this is heating up, grate 8 to16 oz of jack cheese. Dip corn tortillas in the enchilada sauce for about 45 seconds to soften them up. One at a time, put the sauced tortillas in a ceramic casserole dish and roll in the Jack cheese and shredded chicken.. Stack them in the casserole dish until it is full and top with black olives and grated jack cheese.

    Bake at 350° for about 45 minutes until the cheeses is melted to perfection. Serve with Spanish rice and beans and garnish with cilantro, sour cream, avocado and chopped tomatoes.

My Dad can sure make a great succulent roast chicken, but what he does with the leftovers is even more impressive. Whenever he cooks chicken, he will save the leftovers and the carcass because this is where some of the most tender and juicy meat of the chicken is, where it hugs the bones. He will always take these benign and meager scraps and transform them into something fresh and flavorful. These enchiladas are a serious hit in our family. You could say it's just been tradition to use the food from last night's dinner to make the next delicious meal. This is probably true for many families. A great cook is a resourceful cook. My Dad has the gift of making something special out of seemingly simple ingredients.

Opposite: Family Photo on the Ranch

Chicken Fricassee

INGREDIENTS:
1 whole cut-up chicken
Seasoned Flour: 1 cup all-purpose
**   flour +1 tsp Kosher salt + 1/4 tsp**
**   ground pepper**
¼ cup vegetable oil
2 tbsp olive oil

2 sliced onions
4 cloves of garlic, minced
1 red bell pepper sliced
1 green bell pepper sliced
1 15 oz can Italian plum tomatoes
2 cups chicken stock
Saffron (2-3 threads)

DIRECTIONS:

Place the seasoned flour in a large brown paper bag. Wash and pat dry the chicken pieces, sprinkle with salt and pepper. Place all chicken pieces in the bag of flour and shake to coat well

In a large skillet, brown the chicken pieces in 2-4 tablespoon of vegetable oil, adding additional oil as needed Remove the chicken pieces, add another 1 tbsp of olive oil. Add the onion, red and green peppers and sauté until tender and lightly browned. Add the garlic and sauté another minute. Return the chicken to the pan and add the plum tomatoes, chicken stock, and saffron. Bring to boil and reduce to simmer for 45 minutes covered.

Season with salt and pepper to taste.

Dad's chicken fricassee recipe smells wonderful as he prepares it! It is an especially easy one pot meal to prepare and served with long grain rice and a salad, it makes a great family meal. Leftovers make a fine lunch the next day. The peppers are especially delicious. You may add a little white wine or cream if you wish, but we just make it the way it is written.

Chili Rellenos with Panko

CHILI RELLENO INGREDIENTS:
1 box Japanese Panko bread crumb
  mix, seasoned with salt and pepper
6 poblano chilies, roasted with skins
  peeled and seeds removed*
1 lb Monterey Jack cheese
Egg Dip: 3 egg whites + 1 egg beaten
Olive oil to drizzle
1 bunch cilantro

RED SAUCE INGREDIENTS:
1 medium onion, chopped
2 tbsp olive oil
4 plum tomatoes, chopped
2 cloves, garlic minced
½ tbsp cumin
½ tbsp oregano leaves
½ tsp ground chile
2 dried red chile, seeded and chopped**
1 cup chicken or vegetable broth
Salt / pepper to taste

CHILI RELLENOS DIRECTIONS:

Pre-heat oven, 375°. Stuff the poblano chile with a slice of the Monterey jack cheese. Dip the whole chile in the egg dip, then into the panko crumb mix. Place in baking dish. Drizzle olive oil over the chilies. Bake in the oven for 40-45 minutes until crispy and brown and the cheese is bubbling. Serve topped with red sauce, below, and fresh cilantro sprigs.

RED SAUCE DIRECTIONS:

Saute onion in olive oil over medium heat until carmelized and brown, about 5 minutes. Add chopped tomatoes, sauté another 2 minutes. Add garlic, spices, and red chile and sauté for 1 more minute. Add remaining ingredients, bring to a boil, and simmer for 30 minutes. Cool, taste and season, and puree in a blender until smooth.

*Roasting Peppers is an easy way to bring fresh peppers to any recipe. Simply turn the gas burner to high and with the use of tongs, place the pepper on the open flame. (Turn your hood ventilator on and open your kitchen windows as well or your smoke alarm is sure to go off!)

**Dried Red chilies have always been brought to our house from Dad and Mom's trips to Santa Fe, New Mexico where they always return home with fresh, bright red chili ristras in the Fall. We used them to decorate our home during the holidays but later watch them dry into a beautiful magenta color. Whenever we want a dried red chili, we just pick one off the ristra hanging outside. If you don't have a ristra, dried red chilies can be purchased at the market in the Southwestern/ Mexican food specialty sections.

Chili Verde

INGREDIENTS:
3 lb pork butt or pork shoulder, cubed
Seasoned flour (1 cup all-purpose flour
   with 1 tsp Kosher salt and ¼ tsp
   milled pepper)
½ cup vegetable oil
2 tbsp olive oil
2 onions sliced
4 tomatillos, diced

2 anaheim chiles, roasted and peeled,
   seeded, and sliced
2 poblano chiles, roasted and peeled,
   seeded, and sliced
2 plum tomatoes diced
4 cloves of garlic, minced
1 tbsp cumin
1 tbsp oregano
Chicken stock

DIRECTIONS:

    Sprinkle the cubed pork with salt and pepper. Place seasoned flour in a brown paper bag and place all the pork into the bag. Shake the bag to coat the pork pieces. In a large soup pot, brown the pork pieces, a few pieces at a time in the vegetable oil. Remove the pork and drain in a bowl with a paper towel. Place the onions in 2 tbsp of olive oil and sauté until carmelized. Add the tomatillos, chilies, and garlic, stirring frequently. Add the cumin and oregano, mixing frequently. Return the pork to the pot and add the chicken stock—enough to cover the ingredients. Bring to boil, then turn down to simmer for 1½ hours. Serve over long grain rice with chopped cilantro and avocado slices.

    This is one of the most popular family, one-pot meal my Dad makes! He takes pride in how inexpensively he can prepare a meal such as this one. Who would want to go out to dinner after having this spicy richly flavorful stew served atop long grain rice. He often begins this dish in the late morning and lets it simmer through lunch and the afternoon — the aroma of the roasted chilies and the stew is unbelievable. We all can hardly wait for dinner.

    The flavor of the dish improves with time and actually gets better and spicier with time. Any leftovers may be frozen in 1 or 2 serving portions and used for another dinner. I learned to make this for my college roommates, making my house a popular one when the chile verde was being prepared. Served with corn tortillas, a vegetable, long grain rice, and a salad, the only other thing one would need is a cold beer!

Cioppino

INGREDIENTS:

2 medium onions, chopped finely
2 heads of garlic chopped finely
3 tbsp olive oil
1 tbsp thyme
4 cups of water or seafood broth
1 lb of white fish
1 lb of clams

1 lb of mussels
1 lb of peeled and deveined shrimp
Lobster tail and shells
1 15 oz can of chopped tomatoes
½ cup chopped fresh Italian parsley
3 yukon potatoes cut into small ½ cubes

DIRECTIONS:

In a large saucepan, heat the olive oil and sauté the chopped onions for 5-7 minutes until golden brown. Add the chopped garlic, thyme, and sauté another 2 minutes. Pour the water or seafood both into the pan and bring to a boil. Add the Yukon potatoes and cook 10 minutes with a medium boil. Add the tomatoes and cook another 2 minutes. Add the white fish clams, mussels, shrimp and lobster tail and shells and poach the seafood with a low boil for 4 minutes or until the shell fish shell opens. Season with salt and pepper and sprinkle with the fresh parsley.

This is a quick dinner and the shellfish adds richness and flavor to the broth. Serve with fresh French bread and you have a one pot meal. Leftover fish from the seafood market works well and various types of seafood may be substituted.

Classic Meatloaf

INGREDIENTS:

2 lb lean ground round (ground turkey may be used instead)
2 eggs, beaten
1 cup plain, unseasoned breadcrumbs
¼ cup ketchup
½ medium onion, finely grated
1 medium carrot, finely grated

½ green bell pepper, finely chopped
1 tsp kosher salt
½ tsp pepper
tbsp Worchester sauce
2 sliced mushrooms
Browning liquid

DIRECTIONS:

Preheat oven 350°. Mix all the ingredients except the mushrooms and browning liquid by hand. Shape into a loaf on a roasting pan or place in a loaf pan. Pour about 1 tbsp of the browning liquid over the meatloaf and using your fingers, cover the meatloaf with the liquid. Top with the sliced mushrooms decoratively. Bake for 1 hour. Serve with homemade mashed potatoes.

This is a great family dinner and the leftovers make fantastic meatloaf sandwiches to take for lunch the next day. I vaguely remember my Dad making meatloaf in the shape of Mickey Mouse's head when I was younger. It's funny to think back on, because you are told to not play with your food as a kid and I now realize that cooking is a great way to play with your food. Since then my Mom has surprised us all by making a meatloaf in the shape of our dog Gus's head!

Corned Beef and Cabbage

INGREDIENTS:
1 3 to 5 lb bag of corned beef, seasoned
6 white boiling potatoes
6 large carrots, peeled and sliced thick
1 head of cabbage, cut in wedges
2 tbsp Rye seeds
German style mustard

DIRECTIONS:

In a soup pot, empty the contents of the corned beef and seasoning and cover with about 6 cups of water. Bring to boil, then reduce heat and simmer the corned beef for about 1½ hours. While the corned beef is simmering, peel the potatoes and boil about 25 minutes until firm but cooked. Remove from the pan and cool the potatoes in cold water. Place the carrot slices and wedges of cabbage in a vegetable steamer and sprinkle with the rye seeds. Steam the carrots and cabbage for about 15-20 minutes or until firm but cooked. To serve, arrange the cabbage, potatoes, and carrots attractively on a platter. Slice the corned beef and also arrange on the platter. Serve with a great beer and mustard.

This is another great family meal and you don't have to wait until it is St. Patrick's Day to make it!! It is very affordable and healthy (providing you have a lean corned beef) and the leftovers make the most fantastic sandwiches on fresh rye bread. My Dad especially enjoys sautéed corned beef and eggs in the morning. With the time it takes to simmer the beef and all the delicious leftovers, it makes good sense to simmer two corned beefs at the same time!

Eggplant Parmesan

INGREDIENTS:

2 medium sized eggplants
Olive oil
1 tbsp dried basil
Salt and fresh ground pepper

Your favorite spaghetti sauce (homemade or in a jar)
3 cups of grated mozzarella cheese
1 cup of freshly grated parmesan cheese
1 bunch of fresh basil

DIRECTIONS:

Preheat the oven 375°. Slice the eggplant approximately ½" thick and arrange on two cookie sheets. Sprinkle very lightly with salt and pepper and dried basil. Shake olive oil over both sides of the eggplant slices and bake in the oven for 25 minutes until lightly brown and soft.

To arrange, select a medium sized casserole pan and place ½ of sauce on the bottom. Layer a couple of slices of eggplant over the sauce, followed by a handful of mozzarella cheese. Sprinkle ¼ cup of parmesan cheese over this layer and ⅓ bunch of chopped basil. Continue with another ½ cup of sauce, eggplant, cheeses, and fresh basil until the last layer. End the last layer with sauce over the eggplant, cheeses, and place the chopped or whole leave basil decoratively on top. Bake in the oven for 30 minutes or until bubbly and hot.

Serve with your favorite pasta or just by itself.

This is a very easy dish to make especially if you use store bought pasta sauce, it really saves time. The eggplant can be made up ahead of time and layered the next day. Or the entire casserole may be organized the evening before and simply heated in the oven the next work day. Another time saving family meal! Don't use too much salt on the eggplant as eggplant can often taste too salty. This is an excellent vegetarian dish and the leftovers make a great lunch the next day.

Grilled Marinated Tofu

INGREDIENTS:

Two boxes of firm tofu

Marinade: **½ cup low sodium soy sauce**

2 tbsp sesame oil

1 tbsp toasted sesame seeds

2 tbsp sherry wine

Pepper

Pinch of cayenne

1 clove of garlic, smashed

1 inch fresh ginger, peeled and chopped

1 scallion sliced

DIRECTIONS:

Remove the tofu from the box whole and slice into 5 equal pieces. With two boxes of tofu you should have 10 even slices about 1½ inches thick each. Place each slice on a paper towel and let it sit for about 20 minutes to drain as much of the water as you can. Pat the water-extracted tofu dry. To make the marinade, mix all the ingredients and then place each slice of tofu in the marinade for 1 hour. Heat the gas grill for 30 minutes on high, then grill the tofu on medium heat. (Spray vegetable oil or Pam on the grill and the tofu as it tends to stick on the grill and can be difficult to flip.) Grill for 2-3 minute on high and flip over to grill the other side another 2-3 minutes.

This is a healthy vegetarian main course dish. We love this with our other Korean foods and it goes well with fresh steamed rice. No need to marinade any more than about an hour.

Grilled Herbed Whole Chicken

INGREDIENTS:
1- 5-6 lb whole frying chicken
Juice of 2 lemons
½ cup olive oil
2 cloves garlic, smashed
½ tsp salt
¼ tsp pepper
1 cup fresh rosemary chopped
Paprika

DIRECTIONS:

Butterfly chicken, splitting the whole chicken down the back vertically and opening the chicken to lay flat, maintaining the chicken in one whole piece. Sprinkle with salt and pepper.

In a medium bowl combine the lemon juice, olive oil, smashed garlic, salt and pepper, and chopped rosemary and mix well. Reserve several slices of lemon to tuck under the skin of the chicken in the breast and leg region. Sprinkle paprika over the chicken and place chicken in the marinade, turning the chicken several times by hand to cover well with the marinade. Marinade for 4-5 hours or even overnight.

To grill the whole chicken:

Turn gas grill on high and heat for 30 minutes. Turn on low and place the whole chicken on the grill. Cook on low for 1 hour turning frequently. Watch the grill to make sure it is not smoking and that the chicken is not burning. Chicken tends to burn if the heat is left on high because of the skin.

This is a great family summer dinner. Keeps the heat outside and because the chicken takes an hour to cook, you have time to relax, set the table and hang out in the backyard with a glass of wine or beer. Waiting for the chicken to grill gives you some great family time before dinner—a time to catch up on the happenings of the day.

Grilled shrimp

INGREDIENTS:
2 lb fresh, large Santa Barbara or Gulf shrimp
Salt and pepper
Juice of one lemon
2 tbsp olive oil
2 tbsp melted butter
1 clove garlic, smashed
Paprika
Wooden skewers soaked in water

DIRECTIONS:

Peel and devein the shrimp. It takes time to remove the shells and tails and then carefully with a sharp knife slice the back (the dorsal surface) of the shrimp to thoroughly remove the dark vein present. Keep the shrimp chilled as you are preparing them. (You may purchase shrimp already peeled and deveined but our Dad prefers to do his own to insure that they are fresh and clean) Rinse the shrimp well with cold water and pat dry. Shrimp are usually salty and this removes some of the saltiness.

Using the soaked skewers, skewer each shrimp on the skewers leaving enough room on each end for turning and handling. Season lightly with kosher salt, pepper, and paprika. Combine the lemon juice, olive oil, melted butter and garlic and mix. Using a basting brush, brush each shrimp skewer well with the lemon/olive oil/butter/garlic mixture.

Turn the gas grill on high for 30 minutes and when ready place the shrimp on the grill. (Alternatively, a stove top griller may be used.) Grill for 2 minutes on each side or until done and shrimp are brightly pink.

Use the freshest shrimp possible and rinse them off. Shrimp are naturally salty so rinsing them removes some of the salt. Make sure not to over salt them as they can get too salty very easily. The bright pink color is impressive and their flavor when grilled is very good.

Korean Barbeque Shortribs (Kal-bi)

INGREDIENTS:
4-6 lbs of English style short ribs (meaty with the least fat possible)
Marinade:
  1 cup of low-sodium soy sauce
  ¼ cup sherry wine
  ¼ cup water
  2 tbsp sesame oil
  3 tbsp sesame seeds, toasted
  2 tbsp sugar
  3 cloves garlic, smashed
  2 inches of fresh ginger root, peeled and chopped finely
  Zest of one orange
  3 scallions, sliced thin

DIRECTIONS:

Fillet the short ribs to butterfly the thick portion of the meat to unfold from the bone but so it remains connected to the bone. This makes the short rib long and thin with the bone at one end.

Combine all the marinade ingredients in a shallow nonreactive, glass or casserole pan. Mix well. Place the short ribs in the marinade and marinade overnight or 4-6 hours.

Heat a gas barbecue to high for 30 minutes and then begin to grill the short ribs. Grill 4 minutes on each side and turn frequently to prevent charring of the short rib. Serve with hot Cal-rose rice and kim-chee.

My Dad tells a funny story that occurred when we were very little. My grandparents owned a Korean Restaurant (my grandmother is Korean). One busy evening my grandparents had to attend a wedding reception and my uncles were given the charge to run the restaurant for about an hour during the dinner hour. It became so busy that my uncles panicked and called my Dad in for emergency assistance. My Dad picked up the tongs and took over at the grill in the restaurant. He had never cooked Korean food before but the customers were very pleased with their meals and extended their compliments to the chef!

I always associate Ossobuco with my Dad. It only seems natural considering he has cooked it for our family ever since growing up in Los Angeles. Reminiscent about this dish, my mouth waters for succulent veal right off of the bone in a savory vegetable sauce over rice. I could always tell when my dad was conjuring up another culinary masterpiece. I can remember coming home from school after cross-country practice. I had just spent the last two hours running through acres and acres of vineyards, working up a voracious appetite. The first thing I noticed when I walked into the house is a penetrating aroma of herbs and caramelized vegetables and meat, pervading every nook of our home. My dad says that the slow cooking process involved in passionately marrying the fresh ingredients is a gradual pyrolysis: the breaking down of the chemical bonds in the tissues of the meat. By allowing the meat, vegetables and liquid of the dish more time to cook, the flavors will truly marry and the meat just gets melt-in-your-mouth tender. Believe me when I say that the hour and a half of slow cooking is seriously worth the wait. This dish is so good you'll be sucking the marrow out of the bones, something you don't have to feel shy about amongst family or the very best of friends. Enjoy one of my favorite family recipes growing up!

Ossobucco

INGREDIENTS:
4 veal shanks with bone
3½ tbsp olive oil
1½ white onions
3 sticks of celery
3 carrots
1½ cups of peeled plum tomatoes
3 cloves of diced garlic
2 tsp of lavender, oregano, thyme, rosemary mixture (herbes de provence)

Salt
Pepper
1 cup of dry white wine
Stock (optional)
¼ cup water
1 tsp potato starch
Lemon and orange zest
Italian parsley

DIRECTIONS:

Take 4 veal shanks and rinse with cold water. Pat dry and place the shanks in a non-reactive ceramic baking or roasting dish. Salt and pepper both sides of each veal shank. Put shanks into a hot oiled deep-sided pot and brown each side. Remove shanks from the pot and add the trilogy: 1½ white onions, three sticks of celery, and three carrots, all diced carefully. Let these sauté for 3-5 minutes on medium heat until softened and begin to brown on edges. Take 1½ cup of peeled tomatoes (preferably plum tomatoes) and add 3 cloves of diced garlicup Add to the saucepan along with herbes de provence (lavender, oregano, thyme, rosemary). Then add 1 tsp salt and fresh ground pepper to taste. Add 1 cup of dry white wine. Heat for another 2-3 minutes while stirring. Return the shanks back into the pot with enough liquid (water or stock) to just barely come to the top of the veal shanks. Bring to a boil, and then reduce to a simmer.

Cover the whole pot and place in a preheated oven at 325°. Leave in the oven covered for approximately 1½ hours and don't open for at least 30-40 minutes so moisture doesn't escape. Check if there is enough water and add water if needed. Take pot out of the oven and let cool on stovetop. When cool, take out shanks and incorporate remaining mixture by stirring aggressively or using and electric hand mixer. Heat up slowly and add ¼ cup water mixed with 1 tsp potato starch to thicken mixture. (Cornstarch will work too). Replace veal shanks and reheat. Garnish with fresh lemon and orange zest and Italian parsley or basil. Serve with your choice of rice, polenta or potatoes.

Pan Fried Pork Chops

INGREDIENTS:
>   **4 to 6 thin center cut pork chops**
>   **1 cup flour seasoned with salt and pepper**
>   **1 egg beaten**
>   **Vegetable oil for frying**
>   **Fresh Rosemary sprigs**

DIRECTIONS:

Wash pork chops in cool water and pat dry. Dip into egg and then dredge through the seasoned flour.

Heat approximately ½ inch of vegetable oil in a skillet, preferably a cast iron skillet. Place pork chops 1 or 2 at a time and fry until each side is brown, approximately 3-4 minutes per side. Add rosemary sprigs in the frying pan for flavor. Remove from the skillet and place in a paper towel lined plate or serving platter. Serve with applesauce..

These pork chops are one of Dad's specialties and they are so good! The oil used is especially important as you must be able to attain a high temperature without burning the oil. Peanut oil is especially good for pan frying as the it has a higher burning temperature than other oils. It is also great for stir frying vegetables.

Pan Seared Gulf Snapper

INGREDIENTS:
2 lb gulf snapper
Salt and pepper
Olive oil
Paprika
Lemon
1 tbsp peanut oil

DIRECTIONS:

Season the snapper lightly with salt and pepper. Drizzle with olive oil and squeeze with lemon. Sprinkle with paprika. Heat 1 tablespoon of peanut oil in a cast iron skillet. Place each piece of snapper in the oil and pan sear for 2 minutes on each side.

Talk about fast food! This is easy, fast, and healthy. You could also do this for salmon or swordfish. Place on top of mashed potatoes or lobster risotto and serve with your choice of vegetable.

The Wolinsky's: Zach, Andrew, Amerian, Lawrence, and Julia

Perfect Paella

INGREDIENTS:

Chicken legs (8 legs seasoned with salt and pepper)
4 to 6 tbsp olive oil
1 onion
2 cups of white long grain rice
1 red bell pepper
2 large plum tomatoes
3 cloves of garlic
3 cups of chicken stock
8 oz of chorizo (Spanish pork sausage)
8 oz of peeled deveined shrimp
1 lb (about 12) of mussels, cleaned
¾ lb squid
Any other seafood you wish to use
Fresh or frozen petite peas
2 tbsp fresh lemon zest

DIRECTIONS:

Take a large saucepan and brown the seasoned chicken legs in about ½ cup olive oil. Add one chopped onion and sauté until it is browned. Then add 2 cups of long grain rice and stir until rice is consistently coated with olive oil. Stir occasionally for 5 minutes.. Add chopped red bell pepper, plum tomatoes, and garlic as well as ¼ tsp saffron and salt and pepper to taste. Saute for another 3-4 minutes. Add 3 cups of chicken stock and chopped chorizo and simmer for 30 minutes until the rice absorbs the water. Check and add liquid if necessary. Next, add the shrimp, mussels, and squid. Add the peas to steam. Cover and simmer for another five minutes. Serve with a garnish of lemon zest and enjoy!

This is a Valencian dish that is traditionally cooked in a single very large cooking vessel called a paella skillet, but my dad usually does it in a large shallow saucepan. He usually cooks this dish on the weekends when there is time that can be given into loving the ingredients together. Cooking the rice changes the nature of the starches on the outside of the grains and toasts it. This helps give an al dente or firm texture to the rice grains. There are so many things that you can have in paella that every bite is so satisfying in its own way; every spoon or fork-full is a little different.

Poached Santa Barbara White Fish with Saffron Risotto

INGREDIENTS:
1½ lbs of local white Sea Bass (or similar fish: grouper, red snapper, or other sea bass)
3 heirloom tomatoes
3 red peppers
1 onion
4 cloves of garlic chopped
Olive oil
Salt and pepper to taste

Saffron Risotto:
1 cup of Arborio rice
2 to 3 cups chicken or fish broth
½ onion
Olive oil
Turmeric
Saffron

DIRECTIONS:

Heat up 2 tbsp regular olive oil in a large skillet. Add chopped onion and red peppers to the skillet and sauté on medium heat until softened, about 3 to 5 minutes. Add chopped tomatoes, diced garlic, a few pinches of salt, fresh pepper, and ¼ tsp saffron. Add a cup and a half of water or fish stock to the mixture, cover and simmer for 20 minutes.

Before you are ready to serve, take fresh white sea bass and poach it in the simmering sauces for about 5 minutes on medium heat. Serve over saffron risotto or fresh french bread with delicious broth.

Saffron Risotto:

Using a small cooking pot, begin by sautéing half of an onion in some olive oil. After about 5 minutes of sautéing, add 1 cup of Arborio rice and stir around until the grains are coated with olive oil. Let the starch of the outer part of the rice cook for 7 minutes on medium heat. Heat up 2½ cups of chicken broth so that it is nearly boiling. After letting the rice cook, add the chicken broth in quarter cup increments every 5 minutes or so as the liquid is absorbed, stirring frequently. (about 25 minutes). Be careful when you first add the broth as it may excitedly boil in the pot. Add ½ tsp turmeric and stir to give the risotto a beautiful yellow color. Add a few strands of saffron and stir. Serve and enjoy!

This lean, light and flakey white fish is in season only certain times in California and is caught just off the coast of Santa Barbara, California. It cooks very quickly and is most delectable when poached in its own broth.

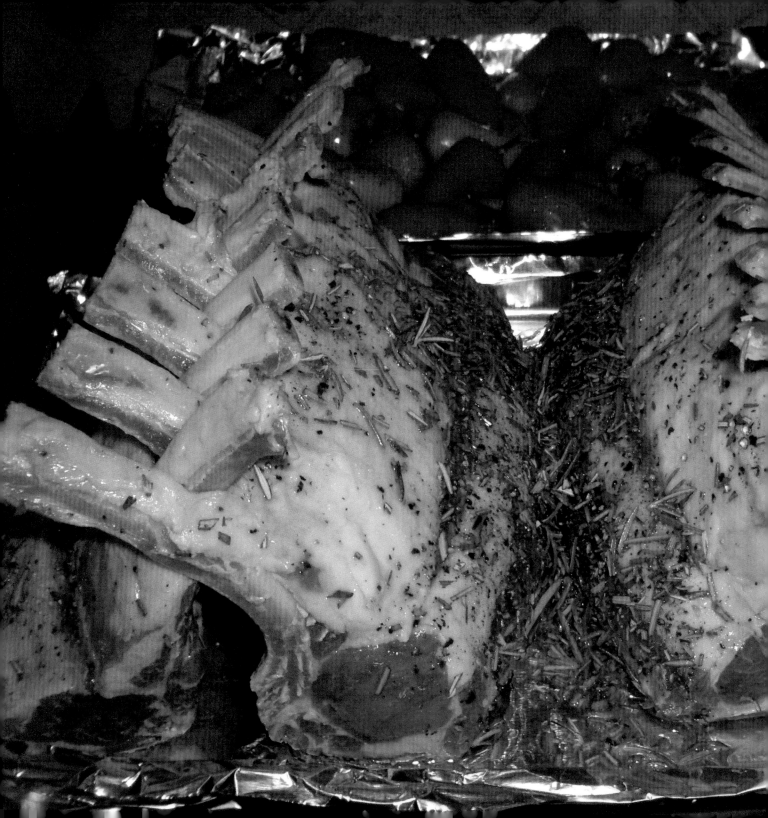

Rack of Lamb

INGREDIENTS:
2 racks of baby lamb
Salt and pepper
Fresh rosemary
Olive oil

DIRECTIONS:

Preheat oven 450°. Prepare the baby back lamb racks by trimming the fat from the bone, leaving the bone free of periosteum. Line a roasting pan with foil and place the racks of lamb in the pan. Sprinkle all surfaces with salt, pepper and chopped rosemary. Place the racks on the roasting pan interlocking the bones attractively. Place in the oven for 10 minutes at 450°, then reduce to 375° for another 15 minutes.

This is a family favorite for holidays and special occasions. Talk about fast food! This only takes about 20 minutes to bake in a hot oven. They are so delicious! The fresh rosemary is particularly good with lamb. Our rosemary bushes grow wild like weeds in the garden. This is an herb you cannot live without and is extremely hearty. It remains productive regardless of the heat and freezing temperatures that we may encounter. It is a must have in the garden!

Roast Pork with Onion / Prune Confit

INGREDIENTS:
3 to 5 lb crown pork roast with bone
1 tbsp kosher salt
1 tsp fresh ground pepper
Fresh rosemary sprigs
Fresh or dried thyme
Hungarian sweet paprika

ONION/PRUNE CONFIT:
2 sweet onions sliced thin
1 cup of pitted prunes
2 tbsp olive oil
1 tbsp butter
Salt and pepper
½ cup of low sodium chicken broth

DIRECTIONS:

Preheat oven 375°. Prepare a roasting pan lined with aluminum foil. Place roast in the pan. Sprinkle with salt, pepper, chopped rosemary and thyme. Do this to the top and undersurface as well. Sprinkle all surfaces with paprika. Bake for 1 hour until brown, basting a couple of times with the pan juices.

Onion/Prune confit:

Heat the olive oil and butter in a sauté pan and add the sliced onions, sautéing over medium heat until the onions are carmelized—about 8-10 minutes. Add the prunes and continue to sauté. Season with salt and pepper and add the chicken stock. Cover with a lid and simmer for 20 minutes on low. Serve this confit with the roast pork.

This is a great family recipe and can be dressed up to make a nice holiday or special occasion meal as well. Leftovers again are great and can be used for tostadas and tacos or even a roast pork sandwich. Dad has a way of making a meal last for several with creative ways for using leftovers. His thrifty philosophy has served us many wonderful, healthy, and affordable meals for our family. Home cooking allows you to do this!

Scallopine of Veal alla Marsala

INGREDIENTS:

1¼ lb of veal scaloppini from the
  top round, cut ¼ thick
⅓ cup all–purpose unbleached flour
Salt and fresh ground black pepper
3 tbsp unsalted butter

2 tbsp vegetable oil
1 lb of brown mushrooms
1 cup of good quality Marsala
2 tbsp chopped fresh parsley leaves

DIRECTIONS:

Thin the scaloppini by placing each slice between wax paper and pounding them lightly. Sprinkle with salt, pepper and flour. Heat 2 tbsp of the butter and the oil in a large sauté pan and add the scaloppine. Cook over medium heat until the veal is golden and toasted on each side and then remove the veal and place on a plate lined with a paper towel. Add the last tablespoon of butter and cook the mushrooms, sautéing them over high heat, mixing frequently until brown.

Add the marsala and mix well, cooking to evaporate the alcohol. Reduce the volume of liquid to half and replace the veal to warm and serve. Sprinkle with chopped parsley.

This is a very quick and fast dinner and may be complimented with either red or white wine. Potatoes are Dad's favorite so this is what he prefers to have with a vegetable like sautéed spinach or red chard. This is a Saturday night favorite.

Seafood Veracruz

INGREDIENTS:

1 lb white fish like halibut or seabass
1 lb medium-large raw, deveined shrimp
12 clams
2 tbsp olive oil
1 tbsp butter
1 medium onion, peeled and chopped

2 celery stalks, peeled and chopped
2 carrots, peeled, and chopped
4 plum tomatoes, chopped
4 tomatillos, chopped
2 poblano chilies, blackened, peeled and chopped
2 cups low-sodium chicken or fish stock

DIRECTIONS:

Heat the olive oil and butter in a large sauté pan with lid. Saute the onions, celery, and carrots in the oil and butter to "sweat" the vegetables about 5 minutes. Add the tomatoes, tomatillos, and poblano chilies and sauté 2 minutes more. Add the chicken stock and bring to a boil and turn to low to simmer for 20 minutes. Just before serving, bring back to a boil and turn down to medium heat but keeping a low boil. Place the seabass pieces, shrimp, and clams on top of the sauce and vegetables, then replace the lid and gently steam for 6 minutes. Season with salt and pepper and sprinkle with chopped cilantro. Served with steamed, long grain rice or my Dad's special saffron risotto.

This is one of Mom's favorite Saturday night dinners. Dad makes a richly flavored sauté and sauce and at the very end, just before he is to serve the dinner, he places the halibut or seabass on top of the simmering stew to poach the fish in the same pan. This produces the most moist and flavorful seafood stew.

Shish-Kabobs (Lamb)

INGREDIENTS:
1-6 lb leg of lamb, butter flied and
   deboned at the butcher, cut into 2
   inch square pieces
Marinade: 1 cup olive oil
         1/3 cup red wine vinegar
         4 cloves of garlic, smashed
         2 tbsp dried oregano

1 tbsp ground cumin
1 tbsp ground cinnamon
2 tbsp chopped fresh rosemary
2 tsp kosher salt
½ tsp ground pepper

DIRECTIONS:

Mix the marinade in a large bowl. Place the lamb pieces in the marinade, mixing well to coat the meat on all surfaces with the seasonings. Marinade overnight or at least 4-5 hours.

Heat the gas grill on high for 30 minutes.

Skewer all the meat on metal skewers. Grill all the lamb about 3 minutes per side. Serve with hot steamed, long grain rice and grilled vegetables.

This family dinner is very special. Served with a nice Greek salad it makes a wonderful family gathering. Everyone can participate and help with the skewering of the vegetables and lamb. We have a large collection of metal skewers but if you use wooden ones, remember to soak them in water otherwise they tend to burn on the grill and the meat especially sticks to them while cooking. Sometimes if the rosemary bush in the garden has strong twigs, we have used the rosemary twigs as skewers to add extra flavor and character to our meal. If you like mint jelly (as Andrew does!) you may serve with mint jelly but the lamb stands alone exceptionally well.

Grilled Swordfish with Fresh Mango Salsa

INGREDIENTS:
2½ lb thick swordfish pieces
Salt and Pepper
Paprika
Olive oil
½ lemon

Fresh Mango Salsa
> **2 ripe mangos, peeled and diced**
> **Juice of two limes**
> **1 red sweet bell pepper chopped finely**
> **1 inch fresh ginger root, peeled and minced**
> **Salt and pepper**
> **2 tbsp fresh cilantro, chopped finely**

DIRECTIONS:

With a very sharp knife (or have the fishmonger do this), slice the swordfish pieces in half horizontally to make two filets from each swordfish piece. This divides the thickness of the fish in half, makes it thinner and cooks more evenly and rapidly. Sprinkle with salt, pepper, paprika, and drizzle with olive oil and lemon juice.

For the salsa, combine all the ingredients, taste, and adjust seasoning as you like. Refrigerate up to a couple of hours to let the flavors mature.

To grill the fish: Turn the gas grill on high for 30 minutes. Place the swordfish pieces on the grill, all in one direction. After 2 minutes, turn each piece 90 degrees to the first location, to continue grilling on the same side for 2 more minutes. Flip each piece and grill another 3-4 minutes until done. Serve with the mango salsa.

This is "fast food" at its finest! Slicing the fish horizontally produces a thin fillet, resulting in a quick grilling time. Dinner is ready in minutes. Serve your favorite rice or potatoes and vegetables with this meal. Turning the fish 90 degrees will give you a beautiful cross-hatched design on the first side grilled. This is fun to make and very attractive.

Shu-Mai

INGREDIENTS:
1 lb ground pork
1 tbsp low-sodium soy sauce
1 tbsp sesame oil
¼ tsp salt
¼ tsp pepper
1 tbsp fresh ginger, peeled and grated
1 clove of garlic, chopped finely
1 scallion chopped thinly
Prepared wonton skins, round or square

Dipping Sauce:
3 tbsp low-sodium soy sauce
1 tbsp rice vinegar
1 tbsp chopped scallion
Dash of cayenne pepper

DIRECTIONS:

Mix all the ingredients except the wontons in a medium mixing bowl. To prepare the shu-mai, with clean hands take a tablespoon of the meat mixture and place in the center of a wonton skin. Moisten the edges with water and seal to make a purse shape or a half moon shape. Continue making the shu-mai until all the meat mixture is used. Shu-mai may be steamed for 8 minutes or pan fried for 3 minutes on each side with 1-2 tbsp vegetable oil until golden brown. Serve with the dipping sauce.

This is definitely a family activity as the shu-mai is fun to make. Even the youngest in the family can make shu-mai and they are delicious as an appetizer. You may also make them with shrimp or ground beef if you wish. The shape and texture of these exquisite little morsels remind me of premature rosebuds.

Spaghetti with Meat (or Meatless) Sauce

INGREDIENTS:

1 lb of lean ground beef or ground
  turkey
1 lb of sweet Italian sausage
1 tbsp olive oil
1 lb sliced mushrooms
1 red bell pepper, sliced thinly
2 jars favorite pasta sauce
1 8 oz can chopped tomatoes

1 6 oz can tomato paste
2 tbsp balsamic vinegar
1 tbsp sugar
½ cup red wine (or a little more)
½ tsp salt
¼ tsp pepper
1 tbsp oregano
1 tbsp thyme

DIRECTIONS:

Saute the ground beef and sausage together over medium heat until done (about 8-10 minutes). Remove from the pan and drain the fat. In the same skillet, add the olive oil and sauté the mushrooms and bell pepper until soft and browned. Add the meat back to the skillet and add the remaining ingredients. Bring to boil and turn down to simmer for 45 minutes. Taste and season as desired.

Cook your favorite pasta as directed. If we have little time, we usually will make cappellini which cooks in 2 minutes. This is a great family dinner and there is always enough for leftovers or extra friends that happen to show up at dinner time. You can make this vegetarian by omitting the meat. The flavors actually develop and improve over the next day.

Steak Tacos

INGREDIENTS:
2 cups of cooked steak (rib-eye, new
   York, or filet mignon)
2 tbsp vegetable oil
2 tbsp chili powder
1 tsp cumin
1 tsp oregano
Taco shells or corn tortillas

1 tsp thyme
½ cup chopped roasted and cooked
   onions, peppers
2 tbsp chopped fresh cilantro
Salt and pepper to taste
¼ cup water or beef broth
Favorite taco sauce toppings (lettuce,
   cheese, avocado, etc.)

DIRECTIONS:

Heat the oil in a skillet and add the cooked meat. Saute for 1-2 minutes then add the spices and chopped onions and peppers. Season with salt and pepper. Add the cilantro, water, and cover with a lid. Simmer for 10-15 minutes to marry the seasoning. Use for tacos with all your favorite side dishes. Delicious, fast, and easy.

Using quality left over grilled steak makes the best tacos! Cost effective, healthy, and easy to make, teen and college age chefs can easily organize a dinner.

Teriyaki Chicken

INGREDIENTS:
One whole chicken-cut up with
  gizzards removed
4 chicken thighs
4 chicken legs

Marinade:
¾ cup of low sodium soy sauce
¼ cup of sherry
3 tbsp of sesame oil
2 tbsp sugar

3 tbsp of water
1 tbsp of toasted sesame seeds
2 scallions sliced thinly
2 star of anise
2 cloves of garlic smashed
2 inch of fresh ginger chopped
1 tbsp dried tarragon
Rind of one orange
¼ tbsp pepper

DIRECTIONS:

   Rinse and pat dry all the chicken. In a large bowl mix all the ingredients for the marinade. Allow to stand for 15 minutes. Place all the dry chicken parts into the marinade, turning the chicken well to immerse the chicken into the sauce. Marinade for at least 4-5 hours or overnight. Bake chicken at 350° for 45 minutes to an hour.

This marinade is easy to make and imparts a delicious flavor to chicken. The orange rind, tarragon, and star anise are optional and give the chicken added flavor. Make a pot of rice with some stir fried vegetables and dinner is done.

Braised Short Rib of Beef

INGREDIENTS:

5 lb of lean English short ribs
Salt and Pepper
6 tbsp olive oil
6 cloves of garlic, finely chopped
3 cups of sliced carrots
2 large onions sliced thinly
6 medium sized parsnips, peeled and
 sliced on the diagonal
6 turnips, peeled and chopped into ½"
 cubes
4 rutabagas, peeled and chopped into 1"
 inch cubes

1-15 oz can of Italian plum tomatoes
 with juice
10 whole cloves
1 6-oz can tomato paste
½ cup chopped Italian parsley
¾ cup red wine vinegar
½ red wine (optional)
3 tbsp brown sugar
Additional fresh ground pepper
3-4 cups of Beef Stock

DIRECTIONS:

Salt and pepper the short ribs and heat 5 tbsp of the olive oil in a large Dutch oven of large casserole pan. Sear the ribs, 3-4 at a time to brown on all sides. Remove them as they brown and stack on a plate lined with paper towels to absorb the oil.

Preheat the oven 350 degrees.

Using the last 1 tablespoon of olive oil, sauté the vegetables, onions, carrots, parsnips, turnips, and rutabagas on medium heat to brown and sweat the vegetables. Add the cloves, tomatoes, tomato paste, and chopped parsley, mixing well. Return the short ribs to the pan and add the remaining ingredients. Add 3-4 cups of stock until the ribs and vegetables are just covered. Cover with the lid and bring the mixture to a boil. Take the pot to the oven and bake for 1½ hours. Uncover and bake for 1½ hours longer or until meat is tender. Season as needed with salt and pepper, then serve. Sprinkle with finely chopped Italian parsley.

This recipe can be made in advance and simply heated up. It is very flavorful with lots of over braised vegetables. If you like you may remove the ribs and puree the vegetables for a slightly different texture to the sauce. We prefer to have the root vegetables to eat as prepared. This heartily serves a crowd!

Veal Chop

INGREDIENTS:
2 to 4 medium veal chops with bone
Salt and pepper
½ tsp Sweet paprika
1-2 cloves of garlic, sliced thin
Fresh rosemary
Olive oil to drizzle over

DIRECTIONS:

Rinse and pat dry the veal chops and trim any fat around the edges. Salt and pepper each side. Chop the fresh rosemary and sprinkle over both sides. Sprinkle with sweet paprika and arrange a few garlic slices on each side. Drizzle both sides with olive oil, rubbing with your fingers to incorporate the flavors. You may let this side for ½ hour while the grill is becoming hot and as you are preparing the side dishes.

Heat an outdoor barbeque grill or a stove top grill on high and lightly oil the grill. Place the veal chops on the grill and cook for 4 minutes. Rotate 90 degrees on the same side and cook another 2 minutes. (This gives the nice cross hatch markings on the first side.)

Flip the veal chop over and allow to cook another 4-5 minutes until done to your liking. Medium will take about 5 minutes for a 1 -1/2 inch thick veal chop. (If you want the cross markings on both sides, then cook for 4 minutes and rotate 90 degrees on the same side and cook another 2 minutes.).

Veal Chop is an elegant dinner and served only on occasion when a great cut of meat can be acquired. The seasonings are minimal which allows for the flavor of the tender meat to be pronounced. Served with mashed potatoes and an onion confit, it is definitely a special Saturday night dinner. Once you learn to make a cross hatching mark on veal chop or steak, you can't resist not making it on all the meats you barbeque. Dad also has a great branding iron given to him to use which brand his initials on the steak he serves. And did you know that the special tool for turning the steaks over can be purchased as a right or left handed? Dad has a special barbeque flipper which is left handed with a horn as a handle.

Dad's Spudworthy Recipes

Baked Potatoes

INGREDIENTS:
One Yukon gold potato per serving

DIRECTIONS:

Preheat oven 375°.

Wash and dry the potatoes, using the freshest potato (without blemishes or eyes!). With a sharp knife, pierce the potato in several areas to allow for steam to escape while baking. Place the potato on the oven rack and bake for 1 hour or until golden and skin is slightly crispy.

Ever have a potato blow up on you in the oven?! This is the reason your potatoes need piercing. That is so that any air internally may escape without damage to their rustic skin, not to mention the mess in the oven when one does explode. A baked potato is the easiest starch and side dish to offer. Make extra for home fries for another meal—either for breakfast or dinner. We usually decide on baked potatoes if the oven is already on for a roast chicken or leg of lamb. We love to conserve on energy and utilize the heat of the convection oven for a one oven meal. This often includes an oven-roasted vegetable as well. Only on a very rare occasion would we turn the oven on for an hour of energy for the lone potato. Our potatoes are always happily roasting with company in the oven.

Opposite: Twice-Baked Potatoes

Classic Mashed Potatoes

INGREDIENTS:
8 Yukon gold potatoes, medium to large
4 cups boiling water in a large pot, salted with ½ tsp salt
1 cup whole milk, at room temperature
1/3 cup butter
Salt and pepper
Paprika

DIRECTIONS:

Peel the potatoes, quarter, and cut the quarters in half so the potatoes are in 8 chunky pieces. Place the potatoes in the water, bring the salted water to boil and reduce the heat to a slow boil. Boil potatoes for approximately 25 minutes until they are tender. Drain the water, sprinkle with salt and pepper and add the butter in slices. Using a potato masher, mash the potatoes with the melting butter and mix quickly as you coat the mashed potatoes with the butter. Add the milk slowly a little at a time and continue to mash. Do not over mash. Using a spoon to mix now, continue to add the milk until the texture is the proper consistency of mashed potatoes. Keep the heat on low at this time. Taste now to add more salt, pepper, or a little more butter to your liking.

The key to great mashed potatoes is the critical timing of mashing the starch (potato) and coating the starch with the fat (butter). If you over mash the potatoes, your potatoes will be pasty and glutenous.

Hash Browns

INGREDIENTS:
3 to 4 large Yukon gold potatoes
Vegetable oil

DIRECTIONS:

Boil the Yukon gold potatoes until you can put a toothpick through them. They should be cooked but very firm. After they are cooked, put them in the fridge overnight. Peel and grate them. Take a palm-sized ball of the grated potatoes and press down flat down on skillet with hot vegetable oil. Add salt and pepper to taste and enjoy!

Goes really well with some good local, humanely treated chicken eggs. You can store the leftover uncooked grated potatoes in the fridge for up to a week, maybe longer depending on your fridge. Or if you have time, make the hash browns and store in the freezer for a later breakfast.

Use large potatoes which do not require peeling. Undercook them so that they are firm when grated and hold their shape. Peel them after they are cooked. These are great to have on hand and may be even prepared for dinner as a side starch.

Potato Latkes

INGREDIENTS:
8 large Yukon gold potatoes
2 eggs
½ grated onion
¼ cup flour or matzo meal
Vegetable oil
About 1 tsp of salt and ¼ tsp of pepper (to taste)

DIRECTIONS:

Peel and grate the potatoes and sprinkle with salt and pepper. Let the potatoes sit for ½ hour. Take a hand full of potatoes and place in a dish towel, wrapping the potatoes tightly and squeezing to remove the water from the potatoes. Continue squeezing the water from the potatoes until all the potatoes have been treated to remove the water content. In a large bowl mix the potatoes with eggs, grated onion, salt and pepper, and flour or matzo meal. In a large frying pan, heat about 1 inch of vegetable oil on high. Place dollops of the potato mixture in the oil to fry. You may fry up to 6 potato latkes at a time but do not crowd the latkes as this will decelerate the cooking process. When the first surface is golden brown, turn over each latke and brown the other side. Remove from the pan and place on a paper towel lined plate to absorb any additional oil. Serve hot with applesauce and sour cream.

Hot potato latkes are reminiscent of holidays and special occasions in our family. At Chanukah, we always make latkes. They are a bit of work but so worth it. Everyone in the family can have a hand in it whether it be grating the potatoes (done with the food processor) or using your muscles and squeezing the water out of them. This is a very important aspect of their preparation as when you fry them, if the water remains, the oil doesn't agree with it and the latkes will not cook properly. If the latkes are made small, they make a lovely and sophisticated appetizer and can be served with a dollop of sour cream, topped with caviar and chopped chives. They also freeze very well so when you go to all the effort, make lots of extras to package in wax paper and seal for the freezer. To heat them up, simply preheat the over 375° and place the frozen latkes on a cookie sheet and bake for 15-20 minutes. They are very special this way as well.

Scalloped Potatoes

INGREDIENTS:
8 large white potatoes, peeled and sliced thin
1 cup heavy cream
3 sprigs fresh thyme
2 cloves of garlic smashed
1 tsp salt and ½ tsp ground pepper (to taste)
Paprika

DIRECTIONS:

In a large saucepan, combine the cream, fresh thyme, garlic, salt and pepper and bring to a boil, then reduce to low. Add the peeled and sliced potatoes and mix well to coat the potatoes with the cream. Cook on low, stirring frequently so that the bottom doesn't burn. Cook for 15 minutes or until potatoes are soft but still firm.

Preheat Oven to 375°.

Butter a shallow but large baking dish and layer the potatoes into the dish. Sprinkle with paprika. Bake for 45 minutes to 1 hour until golden brown.

This is a great side dish and makes enough for the family. The fresh thyme and garlic make for an aromatic and flavorful potato dish. You could add a shallot if you wish as well as some chives.

Twice-Baked Potatoes

See Photo on page 122

INGREDIENTS:
4 large russet potatoes
Salt and fresh ground white pepper
Paprika
Salted butter
Milk

DIRECTIONS:

Preheat oven to 400°.

Wash and pat dry potatoes and pierce the skins of each with a fork so that they can release pressure in the oven cooking process. Put the potatoes in the oven evenly spaced out for about 45 minutes to and hour until skin is firm and crispy, but inside is soft. Take out of the oven and let cool for five minutes.

Cut potatoes in half and scoop out the inside leaving the skins intact. Add ground white pepper, ¼ tsp salt, ¼ tsp paprika, about 3 tbsp butter. Stir together with a potato masher to get the starches covered in the fats from the butter. Once potatoes have a grainy texture, add ½ cup of milk and slowly incorporate the milk, whipping the potatoes with a mixing spoon.

Scoop mixture and put back into potato skins. Top with a little bit of butter and paprika. For fun, use a fork to make criss-cross designs on top. Lay them back on a cooking sheet and put back into the oven for about 10 minutes to brown the tops.

Let cool for 5-10 minutes and serve with sour cream, cheddar cheese, and chives. Enjoy as a side or by itself!

> *Potatoes are versatile creatures that can be used in any number of ways. These twice-baked potatoes are a specialty that my Dad has taught me, but nobody makes them like he does. Imagine potato skin boats filled with creamy potatoes and crisped to a golden brown on top.*

Holiday Homemades

Breadsticks

INGREDIENTS:
1½ tsp active dry yeast
½ cup warm water
5½ cup unbleached flour
1½ tsp kosher salt
1¾ cup of cool water

½ cup biga (see page 139 for recipe)
Additional flour for work surface
1 tbsp unsalted butter at room
  temperature
1 tbsp olive oil for bowl
Poppy or seseame seeds

DIRECTIONS:

In a small bowl, dissolve the yeast in the warm water, set aside until it is creamy.

Measure the flour and salt in a large bowl, add the yeast mixture, the cool water, and the biga. Mix well with a wooden spoon and begin to knead the dough. This will take about 20 minutes to produce a nice elastic, smooth, dough. Mix in the butter and olive oil and continue to knead until smooth. Place the dough in an oiled bowl and cover with a towel. Let the dough rise for 1 hour. Punch down and let rise again for another 1 hour. Preheat an oven 425° F. Roll the dough into a rectangle and with a sharp knife cut into ¼" wide pieces. Pick each piece up and move to the baking sheet, pulling and stretching the stick as you place it on the baking sheet. Continue to do this until you have made as many bread sticks as you can fit onto the baking sheet. Sprinkle with poppy seeds or sesame seeds.

Bake 20 minutes or until golden brown.

(Biga is an easy starter: Mix 2 cups of water with two cups of unbleached flour and 1 package of active yeast. Mix well in a covered bowl and allow to ferment for three days. See page 139.)

These breadsticks are delicious and can be made in such beautiful long whimsical shapes. They are fun and easy to make.

Challah Braid and Birds

INGREDIENTS:
**2 cups of whole milk, scalded and
   cooled to lukewarm (100 degrees)**
**6 tbsp sweet butter + 2 tbsp for
   coating the bread bowl**
¾ cup granulated sugar
½ cup of lukewarm water

2 pkg active dry yeast
6 cups of unbleached flour
2 tsp kosher salt
3 beaten eggs
1 egg for the egg wash
Poppy Seeds

DIRECTIONS:

In a saucepan, heat the milk, 6 tbsp butter, and sugar, stirring to mix the ingredients until the butter is melted. Heat quickly to scald but not to boil. Remove from heat, cover with a lid, and allow to cool until lukewarm. In a large ceramic bread mixing bowl, add the warm water and yeast. Allow to set for 5-10 minutes until the yeast mixture begins to bubble. Add the cooled milk mixture, mixing well with a wooden spoon. Mix in the flour, 1 cup at a time, and after the 4th cup sprinkle in the salt, mixing well.

Add the beaten eggs and continue adding the flour until the dough becomes very still. At this point, it is best to use your hands, dusted with flour to hand-knead the dough directly in the bowl. Continue kneading the dough until the dough pulls together and the entire sides of the bowl are clean. Now bring the dough to the counter dusted with flour and have additional flour ready. Knead the dough for about 15 minutes by hand until the dough is smooth and elasticup Let it rest a couple of minutes and then knead a few more minutes adding just a little flour so that it does not stick. Butter the bread bowl with the remaining 2 tbsp of butter and butter the top of the dough to prevent the dough from drying out. Cover the bowl with a damp dish towel and sit in a warm place to rise for about 1½ hours.

After the first rise, punch the dough down in the bowl and bring the dough back to a flour dusted counter and knead the dough a few times to deflate it. Now you are ready to shape the dough in any form you would like. To braid you may cut the dough into 3 pieces or 6 pieces depending on the type of braid you desire.. Braid the dough and place on an oiled baking sheet. Allow the braid to rise for another 45 minutes. Preheat the oven to 350°. Using 1 or 2 egg yolks with a few drops of whole milk make the egg wash and with a pastry brush, brush the top of the challah. Sprinkle generously with poppy seeds. Bake for 45 minutes until golden brown.

This is a very easy dough to mix and very "user friendly." It becomes a soft and easy to work with dough almost instantly. One of the simple pleasures of growing up was to make a fist and punch down the first rise of the challah bread dough and see it deflate. The dough is living! And the yeast are on the rise. The chemistry of bread and yeast is a great learning topic for children and our mother even hosted birthday bread parties.

CinNand M
(N for Nat and M for Muriel)
Rolls

Challah Cinnamon Buns

INGREDIENTS:
½ challah dough
6 tbsp of softened sweet butter
1 cup of brown sugar
2 tbsp cinnamon
1 cups of golden raisins
1 cup of walnuts, chopped

Icing:
1 cup of powdered sugar
¼ cup of whole milk
Few drops of fresh lemon juice

DIRECTIONS:

Roll the challah dough into a large rectangle: 18 inches long by 10 inches tall or about ½-1" thick. Spread the butter over the rolled dough, leaving the top 2" of the dough without any butter on it.

In a bowl, mix the brown sugar with the cinnamon and sprinkle over the buttered dough. Next sprinkle the raisins and walnuts evenly over the dough. Beginning with the dough closest to you, begin to roll the dough towards the top end, tightly rolling until you have made a tight long roll. Seal the end well, pinching the unbuttered end to seal the roll well. Slice the roll into 3 inch slices and place each cinnamon roll in a buttered casserole dish. Place them about 1 inch apart to allow for the dough to rise overnight.

Cover with plastic and leave in the refrigerator. The next morning, remove the casserole dish from the refrigerator and allow the pan to come to room temperature. Preheat the oven to 350 and bake the rolls for 25 minutes until lightly brown. While still warm, glaze with the icing. Serve warm.

The challah dough makes great cinnamon buns! My mother would divide the dough and make a braided challah for dinner and use the other half for cinnamon buns the next morning. Or you could simply mix in semisweet chocolate chips for a chocolate chip challah or small chocolate chip rolls.

These are really good too.

Challah Croquembouche

INGREDIENTS:

2 cups whole milk
6 tbsp unsalted butter
¾ cup granulated sugar
½ cup of lukewarm water

2 packages of active dry yeast
3 large eggs
6-8 cups of unbleached flour
2 tsp kosher salt

DIRECTIONS:

This is the same receipe as the Challah Braid. Place the whole milk, butter, and granulated sugar in a medium saucepan and heat, stirring constantly until the milk just begins to boil. Remove from the heat and allow the milk to cool to lukewarm or about 100 degrees. In a large ceramic bread bowl, place the warm water and the active yeast and allow the yeast to soften and begin to bubble for about 10 minutes. Add the cooled milk mixture and 2 cups of flour and mix with a wooden spoon. Add the 3 beaten eggs and mix well. Add 2 more cups of flour and mix vigorously. Sprinkle the salt over the dough and add an additional cup of flour. Mix well and dust your hands with flour.

Gather all the dough from the edges of the bowl and bring together. Begin to knead the soft dough in the bowl. Add additional flour as needed to make the dough smooth, elastic, and easy to handle. On the counter, flour the counter top and knead the dough by hand for another 10-15 minutes until the dough is smooth and elasticup Butter the large ceramic bread bowl and place the dough in a warm area of the kitchen to rise for 1½ hours or until doubled. Punch the dough down and form into 1 inch balls. Place on an oiled cookie sheet and make as many balls as possible. Allow the balls to rise and brush with egg yolk and milk mixture.

Bake in a 375° oven for 15 minutes until lightly brown.

To make the Challah Croquebouche: arrange the balls in a tower with tooth picks or cake dowels in a towering pyramid arrangement. It you like you may drizzle royal icing over the tower and decorate as you wish.

The challah dough is a family recipe used for many years and used mostly for a traditional braided Challah made during the Holidays. It is such a versatile dough that many variations on a theme may challenge your creativity. The wonderful smell of this dough is fantastic and the next day it can be used for sandwiches and also makes delicious toast and french toast too.

Ciabatta (Italian Slipper Bread)

INGREDIENTS:
Biga:
2 cups of unbleached flour
2 cups of bottled water

Other:
2 tsp active dry yeast
½ cup warm water, (105 degrees F)
7½ cups of unbleached flour

2 tbsp salt
3 cups of cool water
1 cup of Biga
Additional flour for kneading
Olive oil for the bowl
Medium-grind yellow cornmeal for the baker's peel *(a large wooden paddle, like a pizza paddle, which is used to transfer the raised dough to the hot bread stone prepared in the oven)*

DIRECTIONS:

Biga: The biga is a sourdough starter, very easy to make. Including some of this "biga" starter enhances the flavor, texture and rise of the bread dough. Measure 1 cup of the flour and add 1 cup of water, mix well with a wooden spoon. Cover tightly and let stand at room temperature for 3 days, stirring its down daily. After 3 days, add the other cup of flour and water and stir well with a wooden spoon. Let stand at room temperature for another 24 hours and now it is ready to use.

In a small bowl, dissolve the yeast in the warm water until it is bubbly, about 10 minutes. In a large bowl, measure the flour, mix in the salt, and add the cool water and 1 cup of biga. Mix well with a wooden spoon until the dough is too stiff to mix. Pull the dough together with flour dusted hands and knead it well in the bowl, bringing all the dough together. Later, position the dough on a well floured surface for kneading. Begin to knead the dough, folding and kneading until smooth and soft. This may take up to 20 minutes including some rest periods of 1-2 minutes. Replace the dough into the oiled bowl, cover with a towel and let the dough rise for 1½ hours, until doubled. Punch the dough down folding the edges and re-cover. Let the dough rise a second time until doubled about 1 hour.

Turn the dough back onto a lightly floured surface and divide the dough into two pieces, long and flat.

Let rise 45 minutes. While the dough is rising preheat the oven to 425° F and heat the baking stone (A large flat stone heated in the oven). Spritzer with water, the steam and the hot stone give a crisp crust to breads.) in the oven. Dust a baker's peel with cornmeal and gently transfer the loaves to the peel. With a sharp bakers razor, make three diagonal slashes on the top of the rising loaves. Open the oven and with the quick flick of the wrist scoot one the loaves onto the heated baking stone. Repeat with the second loaves carefully! Bake for 40-50 minutes until golden brown. Remove to wire racks to cool completely.

Opposite is a funny picture of my dad "wearing" freshly baked ciabatta, the slipper bread as if they were really slippers. His sense of humor always kept us laughing.

Clove Studded Oranges (Pomander)

INGREDIENTS:
2 oranges or more
1 cup of whole cloves

DIRECTIONS:

Using the pointed end of the clove, pierce the skin and insert the cloves placing them close to each other until the skin of the orange is completed covered. Allow the orange to dry in a dry area of the house until the orange is completed firm. This may take several weeks. Tie an attractive ribbon around them to hang as an aromatic in your closet or place in your closet drawer.

This is an old fashioned activity for children to engage in during the holidays. The fragrance is wonderful and the oranges make inexpensive and well received holiday gifts which keep for many months if not years to come. They are easy to make and fun for all ages.

Good to put in Hot Apple Cider during the holidays!

Flavored Vinegars

INGREDIENTS:
Red wine vinegar
White Balsamic vinegar
Sherry Vinegar

DIRECTIONS:

Fill a large mason jar with your favorite vinegar. Add your favorite herb which may include tarragon, basil, thyme, oregano, or mint. Berries like blueberries, cranberries, raspberries and pomegranates may also be added along with a clove or two of garlicup Let your flavor selection harmonize together for 1 week and the strain through a funnel lined with cheese cloth. Find some decorative bottles to carry your flavored vinegars and label with festive ribbon and gift cards.

These are wonderful and inexpensive gifts to make. We like to use our oregano and tarragon from the garden to make it extra special. The berries give extra flavor and color. The acid ph of the vinegars chemically extracts the flavor from the herbs and the resultant vinegars are wonderful in salad dressings.

Gingerbread

INGREDIENTS:

2 sticks of margarine	**2 tsp cinnamon**
1 cup brown sugar	**1½ tsp ground cloves**
1½ unsulfured molasses	**1½ tsp ground ginger**
3 eggs	
6 to 7 cups of all purpose flour	**Royal Icing:**
1 tbsp baking soda	**3 cups of confectioners' sugar**
1 tsp kosher salt	**2 egg whites**
1 tsp allspice	

DIRECTIONS:

In a mixer, cream the margarine and sugar, mixing well. Then add the molasses and eggs, beating until well blended. In another medium bowl, shift 4 cups of flour with the baking soda, salt, and spices. Gradually add the dry ingredients to the margarine/egg mixture, blending until mixed. The dough will be stiff. Divide in two, forming two balls, and chill for at least 2 hours. You may also freeze the dough and use at a later time as well.

Preheat oven to 350°. Vegetable spray or lightly oil the baking sheets. Roll the dough into ¼" thickness and hand cut your desired shapes or use cookie cutters if you are making cookies. Bake for 10-15 minutes. Allow larger pieces to cool entirely before removing from the baking sheet.

To make the royal icing, simply mix the powdered sugar with the egg whites, mixing enough sugar until the icing has enough body for piping. Use the royal icing to glue walls together for a gingerbread house or decorate and tint with different colors for cookie icing. The icing sets very hard!

This is a great recipe which we make during the holidays. We often save a little dough to put aside in the freezer to make gingerbread heart shapes in February for Valentine's Day! What at treat that is to find a small ball of dough, ready to roll in the freezer! (Just make sure you label it well so that it can be identified in the freezer.) One of our favorite holiday family activities includes making a gingerbread house and decorating it over a period of several days. Everyone gets to be creative and add their personal touches. We have had gingerbread house parties where our close family friends arrive to celebrate the holidays. The gingerbread houses are already made and each family decorates and takes home a lovely gingerbread house for their own holiday enjoyment.

Seasonal Preserves

INGREDIENTS:
4 lb of homegrown plums
4 lb of homegrown peaches
Juice of one lemon
2 packages of liquid pectin
4 cups of granulated sugar

DIRECTIONS:

      Cut and pit the fruit and place in a large saucepan and begin to cook the fruit. Add the sugar and bring to a boil to dissolve the sugar. Add the pectin and boil for 5 minutes. Check the temperature using a jelly thermometer. Continue to boil until the thermometer reaches the jelly stage. Pour the fruit into clean preserve jars and seal. Boil for 20 minutes to seal the jars.

We have made so much peach and plum jam over the years. Zachary prefers not to use the pectin and boils the fruit until the jelly stage is reached. He does not like to use much sugar and so this process can take a few hours. The results are well worth the wait as his jams are rich in flavor and low in sugar.

Opposite: Sunset at Pismo with our dog, Gus

Sugar Cookies

INGREDIENTS:
4½ cups of sifted flour
4 tsp baking powder
1 tsp salt
1½ sticks of butter
1 ¾ cups of sugar
½ cup milk
1 tsp vanilla

Royal Icing:
One egg white
2 to 4 cups of powdered sugar
Assorted food colors or melted dark chocolate

COOKIE DIRECTIONS:

Sift together the dry ingredients. Cream the butter and sugar until fluffy. Add eggs and beat well. Add the dry ingredients, alternating with the milk. Wrap and chill the dough at least 2 hours. Preheat the oven 375°. Butter or vegetable spray the baking sheets. Divide the dough into quarters and roll one piece at a time on a floured board and cut with floured cookie cutters of your choice.

ICING DIRECTIONS:

Mix the egg white with enough powdered sugar to make a thick but spreadable frosting. Divide the frosting and color as desired. Decorate the cookies as you like and use sprinkles to enhance the decorations. Allow the frosting to totally dry before packaging the cookies.

Melted semisweet chocolate is also an easy way to dress up the cookies. Melt 8 oz of chocolate in a double boiler and hand dip the cookies. Lay the cookies down on waxed paper to set.

Whenever you melt chocolate be careful not to overheat it as it can burn and become very lumpy if it is overheated. To clean the bowl, make chocolate dipped dried apricots by wiping the sides of the pan with the dried fruit. This makes a great added treat and cleans the pan at the same time. We make sugared violets for decoration as well.

Mom and Dad's Desserts

Apple Crisp

INGREDIENTS:
8 tart apples either Granny Smith
  or Macintosh
Juice of one lemon
2 tbsp cinnamon
¼ cup of flour
½ cup of sugar

Topping:
1 cup of flour
1 cup of old fashioned rolled oats
¾ cup of brown sugar
6 tbsp unsalted butter
1 cup of chopped walnuts
Pinch of salt

DIRECTIONS:

    Peel, core and slice the apples, place in a medium bowl, and squeeze the lemon juice over them. Add the flour, cinnamon, sugar and toss to mix well. Preheat the oven to 375°. Prepare a deep casserole dish (9x13 or 8x8) and butter the sides. Place the apples in the dish and prepare the topping. For the topping, combine all the dry ingredients in a medium bowl and then using your hands break up the butter into small pieces to make the mixture crumbly like coarse corn meal. Sprinkle the mixture on top of the apples and bake for 45 minutes until bubbly. Serve warm with vanilla ice cream.

This is a great family recipe and can be made with peaches or plums from the orchard. When these stone fruits are in season, we make a lot of fruit crisps which can also be frozen and heated later as a wonderful dessert. Zachary has been known to make as many as 10 in one day and has also given them away as gifts.

Apple Tart

INGREDIENTS:

8 MacIntosh tart apples, peeled, cored, and sliced thin

Juice of one lemon

3 tbsp unsalted butter

Cinnamon/sugar: ½ cup granulated sugar mixed with 2 tbsp cinnamon

One pie crust recipe:

1½ cup flour

1 stick chilled butter

½ tsp kosher salt

¼ cup or so ice water

DIRECTIONS:

To make the crust: mix the flour and salt and cut in the chilled butter with a pastry blender or two butter knives to break up the chilled butter into the flour until the mixture looks like coarse corn meal. Add the water mixing well with a fork until the mixture just holds together. Do not over mix! The dough will look very dry and difficult to handle but round it up and place on a piece of plastic wrap, gathering the sides to pull the dough together. Chill the dough for at least 1 hour or even overnight.

To assemble the tart, preheat the oven to 375°. Use a 12 inch French tart pan with a removable bottom. Roll out the dough between two floured sheets of waxed paper and roll to a slightly larger diameter than the tart pan to be used. Pick up the dough by holding the edges of the wax paper and flip the dough over the pan, peeling away the waxed paper. With your hands, shape the dough into the tart pan and use the rolling pin to roll over the top of the pan to cut the excess dough, leaving a nicely trimmed bottom crust. Arrange the slices apples attractively in concentric circles into the tart pan. Sprinkle with the sugar/cinnamon mixture and dot with unsalted butter.

Bake the tart for 45 minutes to 1 hour, sprinkling with additional sugar/cinnamon mixture and baste with additional butter. Usually holding a stick of butter in your hand and directly basting the butter to the hot tart works the best. Bake until the tart is richly golden in color.

MacIintosh apples cook quickly and are tart and delicious. They are only available in the early fall and make wonderful desserts. Take care not to overcook the apples as they can become mushy if over done.

These are our family's favorite apples—great for eating as well. Mom has won three first prizes for her apple pie using fresh and firm MacIntoshes in "A Day in the Country" in Los Olivos, California.

We love this tarte and especially like to use our homegrown apricots which are in abundance from the Santa Ynez orchards. They are small and very full of flavor, like nothing you have ever tasted! This tarte is especially interesting because the filling actually becomes cakelike when cooked and absorbs the liquid of the apricots. This process helps make the tarte crisp and delicious and the crust is not soggy from the excessive fruit liquid. My mother has served this for special summer desserts, piano recital refreshments, and school events.

Apricot Tart (Tarte aux Abricots)

INGREDIENTS:
Pate Brisee Au Sucree (Sweet Pie Crust)
1½ cup all purpose flour
½ cup of granulated sugar
⅛ tsp baking powder
**½ cup of unsalted butter cut into pieces
and chilled well**
1 large egg, beaten

Filling:
3 large egg
½ tsp vanilla extract

¾ cup of flour
½ tsp of baking powder
6 tbsp of unsalted butter, softened

Fruit:
**30-35 small ripe but firm apricots, halved
and pitted (Blenheim or homegrown
the best)**
3 tbsp of granulated sugar
**Confectioners' sugar for sprinkling at
the end**

DIRECTIONS:

For the Brisee or crust combine the flour, sugar, and baking powder in a mixing bowl or food processor. Add the butter and cut the mixture together until it resembles coarse cornmeal, then add the egg and stir to combine all the ingredients until the dough comes together. Flatten the dough into a disk shape and cover with plasticup Place it in the refrigerator to chill at least half an hour.

Roll the pastry between two lightly floured wax paper sheets, dusting the sheets as needed. Keep the dough chilled for easier handling. Carefully invert the pastry using the wax paper to handle and move the dough to a large spring form pan. Refrigerate the dough until you are ready with the next layer. Prepare the fruit by cutting the apricots in half and have them ready to go shortly.

Preheat the oven 400° and prepare the filling. Whisk together the egg, sugar, vanilla in a medium mixing bowl. In a small bowl, measure the flour and add the baking powder and stir. Add this to the egg mixture. Add the butter and mix just until the batter is smooth. With a spatula, spread the mixture over the bottom and sides of the crust.

Arrange the apricot halves decoratively in a circular overlapping arrangement. Stand the halves upright and fill to cover the filling. Sprinkle with sugar and bake for 25 minutes. Move to top rack and continue to bake, sprinkling with more sugar and bake until the apricots are golden and slightly browned. For the next 10 minutes, prop the oven door open with a wooden spoon so the steam of the apricots may escape and the dough does not become soggy.

Cool the tart completely and just before serving, sprinkle with powdered sugar. Serve at room temperature with slightly sweetened whipped cream.

Apricots in Marsala

INGREDIENTS:
40 homegrown apricots
4 cups water
2 cups sugar

4 cups Marsala
Cinnamon sticks / 2 per jar
Whole cloves
Zest of 5 lemons

DIRECTIONS:

Bring the water to a boil and dissolve the sugar to make a simple syrup. Add the zest of the lemons. Prick the apricots with a pin and dip into the boiling water just for a few seconds to blanch. Arrange the apricots attractively into the canning jars and fill with ¾ of marsala per jar. Place 2 cinnamon sticks and a few whole cloves in each jar. Fill the jar with the poaching liquid to the top of the jar. Seal with a canning lid and top. Submerge the jars entirely in a large canning kettle and boil for 20 minutes.

These apricots are so delicious and make a wonderful holiday gift in the winter. They are delicious as a topping over vanilla ice cream but equally as tasty by themselves as a simple dessert. (Apricot compote in the jar in the foreground)

Carrot Cake

INGREDIENTS:
2 tsp soda
2 tsp cinnamon
4 large eggs
1½ cups vegetable oil
3 to 4 cups of grated carrots
1 tsp salt
1 cup of walnuts

Frosting
1 8 oz pkg. cream cheese
1 stick butter
1 box of powdered sugar
2 tsp vanilla
Toasted sliced almonds

DIRECTIONS:

Preheat the oven 350°. Sift the flour, soda, salt, and cinnamon. In another mixing bowl, cream the sugar, and eggs until light and fluffy. Add the oil, carrots, and flour mixture together along with the walnuts. Grease and flour a tube or bundt pan and bake 50 minutes or until done. For the frosting, mix all the ingredients except the nuts with a mixer and frost the cooled and chilled cake. Top with the sliced almonds.

This cake has special meaning to my parents as this was the recipe my Mom and her maid of honor, Dr. Ann Sagalyn, used to make a very special homemade wedding cake in 1981. The recipe was actually passed down on a handwritten sheet of school binder paper from my mother's roommate, Margie. The wedding cake is not your typical cake -- it was made in the shape of giant molar tooth! This cake is often requested as a favorite birthday cake. You will see one we made for Dad one year.

Chocolate Bomba Cake

INGREDIENTS:
8 eggs
8 oz best bittersweet chocolate
2 tbsp of espresso coffee
½ granulated sugar
6 tablespoon melted butter

DIRECTIONS:

Separate the eggs into two bowls, one medium bowl for the egg yolks and another clean glass bowl for the egg whites. Melt the chocolate in a double boiler and add the butter and coffee. Beat the egg yolk with the sugar into light in color and smooth. Beat the egg white until stiff peaks are made. Add the melted chocolate, butter, and coffee to the egg yolk mixture. Add the egg whites, folding the whites in slowly and neatly. Butter and line with wax paper a cookie sheet with sides. Pour the batter into the cookie sheet and allow the cake batter to run evenly into the pan. Bake at 350° for 20 minutes. Cool.

To assemble the bomba, line a medium glass bowl with wax paper and cut the cooled cake into strips. Carefully pull the strips out of the cookie sheet and line the bowl. The center of the cake lined bowl may be filled with softened coffee or vanilla ice cream. Place the bowl with cake and ice cream into the freezer until ready to serve. To serve, remove the bowl from the freezer and thaw for 10 minutes. Invert onto the serving platter and decorate with leaves and flowers. You may even serve with a little chocolate sauce of your choice or a fresh raspberry sauce.

This chocolate cake roll may also be made into a lovely chocolate roll. This must be done soon after the cake comes out of the oven. A chocolate ganache or whipped cream may be used as the filling. Place the filling of choice on the lower third of the cake and using the wax paper, pull the cake up and begin to roll the cake. Do this quickly! The filling rolls forward and evenly as you roll the cake. Keep the wax paper on the cake and put the entire roll in the freezer. Later before serving, the wax paper is peeled off and the cake may be decorated with additional whipped cream, berries, or toasted almonds. This is a great flourless chocolate cake. My parents first made this cake when they met in Boston and it is a recipe adapted from a bakery in Harvard Square.

Chocolate Chip Cookies

INGREDIENTS:

1½ sticks sweet butter, softened	**2 cups unbleached all-purpose flour**
¾ cup brown sugar	**1 tsp baking soda**
¾ cup granulated sugar	**1 tsp salt**
2 eggs	**2 cups semisweet chocolate chips**
1 tsp vanilla extract	**1 cup chopped walnuts (optional)**

DIRECTIONS:

Preheat the oven 325° for large cookies and 350° for regular cookies. Cream butter and both sugars together until light and fluffy. Add the eggs and vanilla and mix well.

Sift the dry ingredients and stir in mixing well. Add the chocolate chips and nuts. Scoop 2 tablespoons of the dough and place on oiled cookie sheet. Bake on prepared cookie sheets on the middle rack for 15-17 minutes for giant cookies and 8-10 minutes for regular sized cookies. To make cookies on a stick, have wooden dowels ready to go and insert them prior to baking.

This is such a basic and crowd pleasing recipe. The butter content is slightly less than usually recommended. We have made them for many special and not so special occasions. You really don't need an occasion for this recipe. Making them on stick allows you to present them fancily and also they are fun to eat off a stick!

Decadent Homemade Brownies

INGREDIENTS:
6 oz baking chocolate
1½ sweet butter
4 eggs
2 cups of sugar
1 tsp vanilla
¾ sifted unbleached all-purpose flour
½ cup chopped nuts

DIRECTIONS:

Preheat oven 350°. Melt the chocolate with the butter and cool. Beat the eggs with the sugar and vanilla and blend in well with the chocolate. Add the flour and chopped nuts and mix well. Pour into an 8" x8" greased pan and bake 20-30 minutes.

These are the best brownies and you don't need a mix for these. When you make them from scratch you may trim the fat and sugar a bit and they are still delicious.

Florentines

INGREDIENTS:
3 cups of sliced blanched almonds
½ cup of heavy cream
6 tbsp unsalted butter, cut into slices
¼ cup sugar
3 tbsp honey

⅓ cup of candied cherries, chopped fine
¼ cup candied orange rind, chopped fine
½ cup of all-purpose flour
8 oz semisweet or bittersweet chocolate, chopped

DIRECTIONS:

Preheat oven to 375°. Spread the almonds on a baking sheet and toast them stirring until lightly golden, about 6 minutes. Set aside to cool. In a saucepan, heat the cream, butter, sugar, and honey over medium heat and bring to boil. Boil without stirring for about 5 min until the mixture comes to a temperature of about 150° F. Remove from the heat. Stir in the toasted almonds, chopped cherries, and orange rind then stir in the flour. Pour the mixture into a buttered baking bowl, wrap and let sit in the refrigerator overnight or at least for 1 hour. Preheat oven to 425° and scoop up 2 tbsp of the mixture and place on a buttered baking sheet, spacing them well apart. Take the back of a fork dipped in cold water pat the mixture as thin as possible. Bake until the cookies are golden, 5-6 minutes. Watch them well so they do not burn. While they are warm, gently remove them to cool on some parchment paper.

Melt the chocolate in a double boiler and with a spatula spread the smooth bottom of the surface of each Florentine evenly with chocolate. Use a fork or pastry tine to make wavy lines before the chocolate firms up. Store air tight, up to almost 2 weeks. Makes about 3 dozen.

These are wonderful cookies to add to a holiday gift and they are especially tasty with the orange and cherries included. You cannot buy cookies like these! Other dried fruits may be added but the cherry and fresh orange zest really makes them flavorful.

Macaroons

INGREDIENTS:
1½ cup sugar
5 cups of unsweetened shredded
coconut (purchase at a health food store)
8 large egg whites
Pinch of salt
3 tbsp of unsalted butter, melted

1 tsp of almond extract
1 tsp of vanilla extract
4 oz semisweet chocolate
1 few drops of vegetable oil

DIRECTIONS:

Heat the oven to 350°. Use parchment paper to line a cookie sheet. In a large bowl, mix the sugar, coconut, egg whites, and salt with your hands. Add butter and extracts and combine well. Refrigerate for at least 1 hour. Moisten the palms of your hands with cold water and roll 1 tablespoon of the coconut mixture into a ball and place it on the parchment cookies sheet. Using a spatula, shape the ball to look like a pyramid. Bake the pyramids about 1 inch apart until they are golden brown.

Place the chocolate and oil into a double boiler and melt the chocolate under low heat. Dip the top point of each pyramid into the chocolate and allow them to cool.

These are the most attractive and delicious macaroons you can imagine. The use of unsweetened coconut makes them not so sweet. They are moist and they are definitely my Dad's favorites. We like to make these during the holidays but they are great any time of the year.

Mixed Berry Coffee Cake

INGREDIENTS:
For the Topping:
¾ cup light brown sugar
4 tbsp flour
3 tbsp butter
1 cup of semi-sweet chocolate chips
   (optional)

For the cake:
2 cups of flour

1¼ cup granulated sugar
1 tsp baking powder
½ tsp baking soda
½ tsp salt
⅔ to 1 cup of buttermilk
2 eggs, lightly beaten
1 tsp of vanilla extract
½ cup of butter, melted and cooled
2 to 3 cups of mixed berries, blackberries,
   blueberries, and raspberries

DIRECTIONS:

    For the topping, in a bowl, combine all the ingredients and using your hand mix thoroughly. Mix in the chocolate chips is desired. For the cake preheat oven to 375°. Sift flour, sugar, baking powder, baking soda, and salt together into a medium bowl. In a bowl, measure the buttermilk and add the eggs, vanilla and melted butter and mix well. Add this to the dry ingredients mixing only until the ingredients are smooth. Pour the batter into a lightly greased 8" round springform cake pan. Sprinkle the berries over the cake and then cover with the topping. Bake until well browned, 40-45 minutes.

An old fashioned type of coffee cake is extremely easy and quick to make. You can also use other fruits but the berries really make the cake. It is great to serve in the morning but also can make a wonderful quick evening dessert. My parents once made about 10 of them for a PTA morning meeting. Using loaf pans instead of the springform pans, they were cooled and sliced like bread.

Red Wine Poached Pears

INGREDIENTS:

6 to 8 ripe but firm Bosc Pears
1 bottle dry red wine for cooking
2 juniper pods
1 star anise
Rind of one orange
½ cup sugar
½ cup Crème de Cassis

DIRECTIONS:

Bring all the above ingredients to a boil and poach firm but ripe peeled pears for about 20 minutes. Be sure to leave the long stems on the pears.

Remove pears from the liquid and continue to boil the liquid to reduce until thick, approximately 30 minutes or more to make a thick syrup.   Refrigerate for up to one week.

White Wine Poached Pears

INGREDIENTS:
6 to 8 Bartlett pears: ripe but firm
1 bottle dry white wine for cooking
1 vanilla bean (split the bean and scrape
    the inner pod to remove the vanilla
    essence inside)

2 cinnamon sticks
Rind of one lemon
Juice of one lemon
½ cup sugar

DIRECTIONS:

Bring all the above ingredients to a boil and poach firm but ripe peeled pears for about 20 minutes.

Remove pears from the liquid and continue to boil the liquid to reduce until thick, approximately 30 minutes or more to make thick syrup.

The pears above are very versatile. Dad would use them in salads and mom would use them in tarts. Mom would use the red and white alternating in a tart. They keep well in the refrigerator covered with the reduced syrup for 1 week. Any leftovers are great with vanilla ice cream. The syrup from either makes a great ice cream or yogurt topping. Delicious!

Zach's Santa Ynez Peach Conserve

INGREDIENTS:
50 homegrown peaches, peeled and pitted
4 cups sugar
2 packages pectin

DIRECTIONS:

Carefully peel and pit the homegrown peaches which are usually furry and small. In a large kettle, bring the peaches and sugar to a slow boil and add the pectin. Simmer on low for a long time, about 4 hours, stirring periodically. Cook until the candy thermometer reaches the jelly stage. You must boil off lots of the liquid for this to happen. When the conserve reaches the jelly point, pour into clean and hot canning jars. Seal with the canning lid and boil covered in a deep canning preserve kettle for 20 minutes. Remove from the water and sit on towels to cool. Listen for the ping! (The sound made when the lid seals as the jar cools).

When there is an abundance of fruit, Zach usually comes to the rescue and makes a batch of his Peach conserve. This will use up many pounds of peaches as he cooks and reduces the liquid and fruit to may delicious jars of peach conserve. This process may take days of work in order to harvest all the ripe peaches. He will save this and give it away as Holiday or birthday gifts.

About the Author

Zachary Wolinsky is an alumnus of the University of California Santa Cruz and has a Bachelor of Arts in Anthropology. He is a member and worker-owner of Pedalers Express and Santa Cruz Pedicab; the former a non-motorized bicycle courier cooperative, the latter a pedal-powered bicycle taxi service for Santa Cruz and surrounding areas.

Additionally, he works at the Aptos Farmers Market managing the booth for Three Americas, Inc., a non-profit benefit corporation established to fund projects promoting a better quality of life in the Western hemisphere through the sale of organic, fair-trade, and shade grown coffee. When he is not riding his bike or brewing coffee, he's cooking at home, growing a garden, and playing music.

Also Available from Summerland Publishing

Eat Well With Diabetees

Sansum Diabetes Research Institute
978-0-9824870-5-1
US$24.95

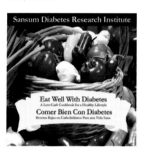

This novel, bilingual cookbook rekindles the joy of cooking - and the pleasure of eating - for those with diabetes and their families. These recipes are also lower in carbohydrate than those found in other diabetes cookbooks. Most importantly, they will leave you feeling satisfied without being deprived of flavor. Enjoy the pleasures of cooking while supporting normal blood sugars and healthful eating!

"Finally a cookbook I can confidently recommend that is truly diabetes-friendly."

Lois Jovanovic, MD, MACE

Tid Bits

Gina La Monica, Ed.D.
978-0-9824870-4-4
US$16.95

Tid Bits is an easy to read picture book of 26 healthy snacks for children. Parents can prepare these snacks in less than 5 minutes. There is even a grocery list at the back of the book to make shopping for these snacks that much easier. With the author being a health professor and exercise physiologist, she provides parents with educational information in the introduction along with educational websites. With the childhood obesity epidemic on the rise, this is a must read for all parents.

Angel on my Handlebars

Patricia Starr
978-0-9795444-8-4
US$19.95

Angel on my Handlebars is the true story of the 50 days it took Patricia Starr to pedal 3,622 miles across America. Patricia was a 67-year-old woman in short shorts and Hanes Pantyhose riding a $600 bicycle with a kickstand and a fuzzy seat cover. All odds were against her. Many of the days during the ride stretched between 100-120 miles.

Patricia Starr is an accomplished concert pianist and was crowned Ms. Senior California at age 69 in 2006, and Ms. Senior Nebraska in 2008.

Lucky Me

Christi Dunlap
978-0-9795444-9-1
US$14.95

"Lucky Me", narrated by a rescued dog named Rocky, provides a guide to children and parents looking to add an animal companion to their family. Illustrated with full color photographs by the author, Rocky and his friends walk us through what a humane society can offer to animals, and what every animal guardian should know about caring for and keeping their new family member safe.

Giving Birth to My Parents

Lorrie Caplan-Shern
978-0-9837923-0-7
US$14.95

Giving Birth to My Parents is a timely book written for the men and women of the Baby Boomer generation by one of their own. Part memoir, part life coaching manual, Giving Birth To My Parents offers a road map to the people of every generation. Its pages offer guidance on how to lovingly and compassionately deal with the sometimes challenging, but ultimately worthwhile, experience of creating and maintaining a loving and respectful bond with aging parents.

All books are available from www.summerlandpublishing.com, amazon.com, barnesandnoble.com, and your favorite bookstore. Email SummerlandPubs@aol.com for more information.